8-23-65

HOBBIES FOR BOYS

HOBBIES

FOR BOYS

by HAL G. VERMES

ASSOCIATION PRESS

NEW YORK

HOBBIES FOR BOYS

Publisher's stock number: 1565

Library of Congress catalog card number: 65-11084

Printed in the United States of America

1323759

"The best fun is in your own imagination."
—ERNEST THOMPSON SETON

CONTENTS

HOBBIES FOR BOYS

1

THE FUN OF HAVING A HOBBY

ONE Saturday morning in midsummer a boy woke up, washed, dressed, ate a man-size breakfast. Getting up from the table, he stretched his arms, yawned, and grumbled, "Ho hum, two whole days ahead, and there's nothing to do!"

Though this boy is a complete stranger to us, there is one important thing we know about him—he doesn't have a hobby! If he had one or more, he would be full of enthusiasm and raring to go. That week end wouldn't be nearly long enough for all the things he would want to do. Maybe in the morning he'd work on a hanging shelf he was making for the shells he had collected while he was on a family trip to the seashore. After lunch, perhaps he was planning to take some action snapshots of a baseball game. In the evening, he would spend an hour or so trying to tune in distant stations on his short-wave radio. Sunday, after church and dinner, the family was driving to another town to visit some relatives, and he expected to trade some stamps with a cousin. Back in the evening, he'd venture out into the night sky with a telescope. Thus every hour of the week end would be crowded with interest, excitement, and pleasure.

Why Have a Hobby?

A hobby, according to the dictionary, is a specialized pursuit that one finds particularly interesting and enjoys doing, usually as a source of leisure-time relaxation. One of the main attractions of a hobby is that it is enjoyable. We engage in a hobby because of the fun we get out of it. And why is it fun? One boy may go in for a collecting hobby; another may feel that collecting things is a pretty dull way to spend the time. A hobby can be fun only if it interests you; and the greater your interest, the more fun you will get out of it.

A hobby also has definite educational value. But don't let that scare you. The pursuit of a hobby is not at all like studying, say, mathematics or grammar at school, which can at times be pretty painful—or at least so it seems. When your dentist pulls a tooth, it may hurt for an instant. But the knowledge you gain from a hobby is absolutely painlessly acquired! Why? Because it particularly interests you, and so you enjoy engaging in it. A hobby, therefore, is a recreation that is interesting, educational, relaxing, and fun.

How to Select a Hobby

The more a hobby interests you, the more pleasure you will derive from it. Thus, to get the most out of it, a hobby should be chosen with care. You probably have one or more hobbies already which, very likely, you took up purely by chance. Perhaps a favorite uncle gave you a postage stamp set at Christmas or on your birthday. You may have worked on it for a while and then, finding that it didn't especially interest you, you put it away. Or a chum built a soapbox racer, so you did, too; but you found that you didn't care much for that hobby, either.

There are literally hundreds of hobbies, and the problem is how to make an intelligent choice of one or more among that vast number. To help you do so is the principal purpose of this book. What interests a friend may not interest you. To try out scores of hobbies not only would take a lot of time, but might well run into quite an outlay of money. To save you both time and money, this book acts as a guide to enable you to select the particular hobbies which fit in with your special personality traits. In that way, you will know—before you invest much time or money—which hobbies strongly appeal to you. And so, when you start on a hobby, you will take it up with interest and in earnest, assured that it is right for you, thus providing you with the maximum amount of enjoyment, knowledge, relaxation, and fun-loving recreation.

How Many Hobbies?

If it is not too limited, one hobby may be enough. For example, still photography can lead to movie photography; short-wave radio listening can lead to "ham" radio operation; and soap sculpture can lead to sculpture in other materials. However, for variety's sake, it is usually better to have several hobbies. In choosing them, select those which contrast with each other. For instance, it is well to have both an indoor and an outdoor hobby, for you can indulge in the first when the weather is disagreeable and in the second when the weather is good. Besides, this plan keeps you from staying indoors too much. Collecting stamps or coins is an excellent additional hobby for evenings when you are tired from some outdoor activity of the daytime and you want something restful to relax you before hitting the pillow.

Therefore, balance your hobbies with active and inactive pursuits. If one hobby is, say, tennis, it obviously would not be wise to take up mountain climbing, too. Neither would you collect stamps, coins, and Indian relics, all at the same time; one hobby in the collecting field is enough. Select hobbies from different fields, but don't go in for too many at one time because, in spreading your interests around, you won't accomplish much with any one of them.

How to Use This Book

First, read this book through from beginning to end, not skipping any chapter; for you want to get a good general view of the almost limitless area of interesting hobbies. Then go back and reread the chapters on the particular subjects that look promising to you. The popular hobbies are described in detail, and those in each chapter are related in one way or another. Discover what you can expect to derive in relaxation, pleasure, and knowledge from a certain class of hobbies. Note the cost of equipment and supplies. Then select the particular one in a field that really arouses your interest and curiosity. Choose two, perhaps three, contrasting hobbies. Then start with the one you think you will like most. Suggestions and full directions are given so that you can begin right away. Try it out for a month or so to see how you really like it. Then if you wish to continue, make a list of the reference books given that relate to that hobby, and get one or more from your public library or a bookstore.

Now you are on your way. Go easy on cash outlay until you are sure that the hobby will serve to enrich your life by making it more interesting and enjoyable. You may continue with the hobby into adulthood and through the years. Or, as you grow older, and your interests change, you may find that you have outgrown it. In that case, don't drop it until you have made another selection and have replaced it with a new hobby which fits in with the growth of your personality and the development of your character. By using this book, you will widen your horizons as you explore the wonderful world of hobbies, which is full of excitement, adventure, and fun.

2

LET'S COLLECT SOMETHING

OF ALL hobbies, the largest and most varied number are in the field of collection. People just naturally like to gather and keep things, and what they select ranges widely into almost anything you can think of. Many people collect string or rubber bands; and if you asked them why, they wouldn't know. Others collect minerals, shells, buttons, valentines, picture postcards, books, prints, match books, glass, clocks, bells, menus, lamps, arrowheads, toy banks, and what not. They are the true collectors, because their collections are interesting and meaningful.

What is the fascination of collecting which makes it so popular? Actually, it is the pleasure derived from searching for something, and the thrill of accomplishment when it is found. It springs from the spirit of adventure, which is a natural characteristic of all mankind. Life itself is a continuing search for certain aims and desires. Thus, a collecting hobby fulfills a definite need.

The pursuit of a collecting hobby is exciting. In collecting Indian head pennies, for example, you may spend months, perhaps years, hunting for one of a certain year. And the longer you have to search, the more the enjoyment when you finally find it. Thus, collecting something that interests you is fun.

Everyone might well be a collector in addition to his other hobbies. It gives you an extra interest in life, and so helps to avoid boredom. It is a pleasant and relaxing pastime. In addition, collecting provides a constant challenge as you continue to look for certain items to build up your collection. Meanwhile, it is educational, for you unconsciously absorb knowledge as you go along. A mineral specimen is just another piece of rock to the layman. But to the collector it has a fascinating story to tell of the millions of years it has taken to form the earth's crust.

If you are really interested in the collection hobby you have selected, its fascination never becomes less. In fact, it increases over the years as you develop a good collection. If you use care and good judgment in building up your collection, it may one day be worthy of exhibit at a club, the public library, or a hobby show; and perhaps you will have the additional pleasure of seeing it written up in your local newspaper.

The two primary factors which determine the satisfaction and success to be derived from a collection hobby are selection and specialization. If the hobbyist does not specialize, he will never have more than a haphazard collection of little interest and value. So collect something which particularly appeals to you, and be specific about your field of interest. The basic rule to keep in mind is that a specialized collection is of much more interest and value than one which is general in character. A collection of cuckoo clocks is more interesting than a collection of just any kind of clock. An album of United Nations

stamps would be more important than a haphazard as-
sortment of all kinds of postage.

How to Collect Stamps

By far the most popular collection hobby is philately
(pronounced fil-lát-ely)—that is, the collection of postage
stamps. Interest in collecting stamps has increased tre-
mendously ever since the first government-issued stamp,
the "Penny Black" of Great Britain, picturing Queen Vic-
toria, was placed on sale May 6, 1840. Today there are
tens of millions of stamp collectors all over the world.
There are a number of factors which make philately a
fascinating hobby: most stamps are colorful and beautiful examples of the engraver's and lithographer's art; they
are pictures in miniature, small enough to be easily
mounted in an album, thus making a collection compact
and simple to display; they are educational since most
stamps illustrate a famous personage or some historical
event; the field is unlimited, millions of different stamps
having been issued all over the world; and finally, anyone
can begin a modest stamp collection at little cost.

In starting a stamp collection, the first thing to do, of
course, is to buy some stamps. Most people just go out
and purchase a packet of a thousand stamps from all over
the world, costing a few dollars. However, this is not the
way to become a good philatelist (remember, accent on
the "lat" here, too) with an interesting collection. In buying "just any old" stamps, you will end up with an album
much the same as that of thousands of other collectors.
Besides, you will be wasting time and money and, most
important of all, you won't get half the pleasure that you

should out of a really wonderful hobby. So, before you begin, look carefully into the field, and study the many varieties of stamps which are readily available. Do not invest any money until you have definitely decided which type of stamps you would like to collect. This decision is the most important one that you will make as a philatelist, and it poses some very interesting problems. Below are recent suggestions made by various stamp dealers. They do not agree, which is important because, if they all said the same thing, everyone would collect the same class of stamps, and so the pleasure of selection and search would be lost.

Collect foreign stamps from the Western Hemisphere: Canada, Mexico, Central and South America. These stamps are readily available and inexpensive.

•

An amateur philatelist might well begin by collecting stamps from the many new, independent countries in Africa. He will have to be on his toes to keep up with the frequent issues that appear.

•

Collect stamps from the country of your ancestry. If, for example, they came from France, you might have relatives there with whom you can exchange stamps. And it would also be of some help if you wanted to learn the language.

•

Collect United States stamps only. They tie in with the history of your country, and they cost very little.

Dealers agree in one respect: they all approve of specializing in the collection of United States commemoratives. These stamps, as you know, are larger than the regular run of stamps, thus permitting a more decorative design. And while you are collecting used (cancelled) past issues, you might at the same time start a collection of new mint (uncancelled) commemoratives as they are issued by the Post Office Department. Since a current regulation limits special stamps to fifteen in any one year, the cost should be only around a dollar, depending upon the face value (that is, whether they are one cent, four, five, fifty or what-not cent stamps).

In order to be advised when new stamps are being issued, subscribe for the posters which describe and illustrate in enlargement the new stamps before they come out. The address is: Superintendent of Documents, U.S. Government Printing Office, Washington, D.C. 20402, and the cost is $1.50 a year. Before ordering, you can, if you wish, go to any post office and look at these posters, which will be found on the bulletin board. The posters themselves, which are interesting and decorative, can be placed in a scrapbook or used as unusual and distinctive wall decorations. In collecting mint commemoratives, since the yearly expenditure is so low, you might consider purchasing them in blocks of four which, over the years, will eventually become a distinctive collection that you can well be proud of.

Most philatelists collect used stamps since they are easier to obtain and much less expensive than mint stamps. However, a small collection of new stamps, which have not been defaced by cancelling, is noticeably more unusual and attractive than a large collection of used stamps. Though you will very likely begin by assembling cancelled stamps, it is, at the same time, a good idea to start building up a modest album of foreign mints. There are two ways to obtain them. One is to write to stamp dealers in other countries, tell them what you are looking for, and what you want to spend.

A simpler, less costly way, is to exchange stamps with foreign correspondents. You might correspond with a boy —or for that matter, a girl—of about your age to exchange interesting information concerning your respective countries. If you are a stamp collector, you can also suggest that you would be happy to exchange mint stamps of your own country for those of approximately equal value from your correspondent's country. If your pen pal agrees, you can then send him about a dollar's worth of new U.S. stamps purchased from your local post office, and look forward to receiving a selection of current stamps from him in return. This is an interesting responsibility because it makes it necessary for you to use both good judgment and good taste in choosing a nice selection of stamps for him; and, in turn, he is challenged to do as well for you.

In starting a stamp collection, don't purchase more supplies than you actually need. After deciding upon and buying the kind of stamps you feel that you want, then purchase an album appropriate for that type of stamp. In addition, you will need stamp hinges and stamp tongs, so that you can handle your stamps with care. Another valuable help is a magnifying glass so that you can examine the stamps for any faults, and also more fully appreciate and enjoy their artistry. This starting set, including the stamps, can be bought for under ten dollars. Later you will want a stamp catalogue in order to know what stamps have been issued and when, and their list value. And as you become more knowledgeful of the variations in stamps, you will want to get a watermark detector and a perforation gauge; but these are not at all necessary in the beginning.

Should you expect that your stamp collection will increase in value so that, later on, you can, if you wish to dispose of it, sell your album at a profit? The firm answer is definitely no. In spite of whatever you may hear or read, the only people who make any money on stamps are the dealers; this is legitimate, for that is their business. In order to make a reasonable profit above overhead, the best that a dealer can offer you for your stamps is half of their listed catalogue value. And even if you have U.S. mint stamps, the most you can expect is ten per cent less than what they cost you. Stamp collecting is a very rewarding hobby, but its values—interest, education, recreation, relaxation, and plenty of fun—are not measurable by money. As such, the hobby is well worth whatever amount you spend on it, according to your means. In later years, you may, if you wish, pass your stamp album on to a son, who will thus have the advantage of a good, basic collection which he can then enlarge. You will have had countless hours of fun, and he will, too, which is the fundamental purpose of any hobby.

Suggested Paperback Books:

Postage Stamps of the United States, 1847-1961 (Government Printing Office, Washington, D.C. 20402), $1.25

A Guide to Stamp Collecting, Prescott Holden Thorp (New York: Minkus Publications, Grosset & Dunlap), $1.00

Stamp Collecting, Merit Badge Library (Boy Scouts of America), 35 cents

Fell's Official Stamp Guide, Franklin R. Bruns, Jr. (New York: Cornerstone Library, Inc.), $1.00

Hobby Handbook 1: *Collect Stamps,* Larry Freeman (Watkins Glen, N.Y.: Century House Americana), $1.25

Suggested Hard-cover Books:

My Hobby Is Collecting Stamps, Ernest Kehr (Chicago: Children's Press), $3.95

Stamp Collecting, Frank Cetin (New York: G. P. Putnam's Sons), $2.95

How to Collect Coins

Running a close second to stamps as a popular hobby is numismatics (accent on the "mat")—that is, the collection of coins. Generally, the basic rules in stamp collecting are also applicable to coins: build an unusual and interesting collection by specializing in not more than a few types of coins—just one is enough for a beginning; start modestly, and spend no more than is needed until you are sure that you will enjoy being a numismatist (accent on the "mis"), and know just what coins you would like to collect; finally, do not expect that you will make a profit from your collection, no matter how long you may keep it.

Hobbies, it cannot be overemphasized, are indulged in for recreation, relaxation, the acquisition of knowledge, enjoyment, and pure fun.

There is one principal difference between the collection of coins and stamps that you should thoughtfully consider before deciding which you would prefer. In philately, the main distinction in stamps is that they are either mint (new) or used (cancelled). Such other differences as perforations and watermarks are only of concern to the serious collector. In numismatics, however, coins are evaluated in seven conditions, which naturally affect their worth:

1. Proof—a specially struck coin issued by the Mint for collectors.
2. Uncirculated—an ordinary coin as it comes from the Mint.
3. Very fine—slightly used.
4. Fine—lettering clear, but slight signs of wear.
5. Very good—worn but still clearly legible.
6. Good—worn but with part of the design still plain.
7. Fair—considerably worn.

"Proof" and "uncirculated" are readily recognizable, but it takes an expert to distinguish between the other five classifications. In fact, to be certain of a coin's condition, and thus estimate its market value, the average collector should go to a dealer for a professional evaluation. Meanwhile, as a beginning numismatist, select the best-looking coins you can find until you have developed a practiced eye with which to determine their standard condition.

As with philately, the first thing to do is to make an intelligent selection of the type of coins you would like to collect. And, as in stamps, the choice is wide and varied. Indian head pennies are the most common coins collected by young numismatists. A "Whitman's board" to hold them is obtainable for thirty-five cents. The only other equipment you need is a coin catalogue describing coins and giving the prevailing list price, and a magnifying glass for the identification of coins and the determination of their condition. Your entire outlay at the start will be five dollars or somewhat less. In order to get going, you will need to examine carefully every Indian head penny that passes through your hands; and you will also want to look at those from the pockets and purses of the other members of your family. At first, don't be concerned with the condition of the coins because your immediate purpose is to get as many coins of different years on the board as soon as you can. Then, as it starts to fill up, replace worn pennies with others in better condition, remembering that it is better to have a small collection in at least "fine" or "very good" condition than a larger collection of coins which are considerably worn, and can be rated as only "fair."

In any collecting hobby, don't be impatient and hasty in trying to build up a big collection; this is particularly true in numismatics where the condition of coins is of such great importance. And don't get the mistaken impression that you can fill up a board with Indian head pennies in a week, a month, or a year. The truth of the matter is that today it is impossible to build up a complete collection of Indian head pennies just by searching for them among circulated coins. The only way to fill out the collection is to purchase the rare items from dealers, which would cost in the neighborhood of three hundred dollars!

So be modest in your aims, as in any other hobby. Without spending a lot of money, you can develop some very interesting and unusual coin collections at little cost. Remember these basic rules: specialize in certain coins within a limited field; hunt for whatever you can find to get started; then replace the poorer specimens with coins in better condition, thus upgrading the set.

Be original and selective in your choice of coins for collection. You could spend a lifetime just collecting U.S. pennies, and still be missing many of the older coins which have become rare. Instead of trying to cover so wide a field, make up small sets which can be completed within a reasonable length of time. An interesting idea, for example, is to collect coins that were minted the year you were born, thus having special significance to you. Try to get one of each, in at least "fine" or "very good" condition, all the way from a cent up to a silver dollar. This set of six coins can be mounted, framed, and hung on the wall, making an unusual conversation piece. You can do the same for other members of your family or good friends, a set with their birth year making an appropriate birthday gift.

Most Americans naturally collect U.S. coins, but you might consider making up a representative collection in the foreign field. Their current coins are not expensive and, by planning to have a half-dozen from each country, it would not be difficult to build up a very nice collection of coins from around the world, which would be different from the usual collection of U.S. pennies, nickels, and dimes. In collection hobbies, use your imagination and develop modest collections that have some special significance, and that show originality, thought, and care on your part. The distinction of any collection, whether it be stamps, coins, or what have you, does not depend upon its size, but rather upon the time, work, and good judgment that you have put into it.

Suggested Paperback Books:

Coin Dictionary and Guide, C. C. Chamberlain and Fred Reinfeld (New York: Barnes & Noble), $1.50

Coin Collecting, Robert V. Masters and Fred Reinfeld (New York: Sterling Publishing Co., Inc.), $1.00

Coins and Coin Collecting Made Simple, Laurence Brown, Made Simple Books (Garden City, N.Y.: Doubleday & Co., Inc.), $1.45

Collectors' Guide to Standard U.S. Coins, Herbert Ferguson (New York: Bantam Books), 60 cents

Fell's International Coin Book, Jacques Del Monte (New York: Cornerstone Library, Inc.), $1.00

Coin Collecting, Merit Badge Series (Boy Scouts of America), 35 cents

Suggested Hard-cover Books:

Coin Collector's Handbook, Fred Reinfeld (New York: Sterling Publishing Co., Inc.), $2.95

Collecting All Sorts of Things

The things you might collect are limited only by your own imagination. In selecting a specific collection hobby, make it a practice to keep an eye out for items which particularly hit your fancy. This is very important because it is the degree of your interest which makes a hobby pleasurable and rewarding. A collection hobby should fit in with your personality and way of life. Perhaps you would like to hunt for Indian arrowheads, and another fellow would want to collect mechanical banks. Look over the various collecting hobbies given below, and consider whether or not any one of them appeals to you.

Autographs

Many young people have a fling at autograph collecting by getting the signatures of classmates when graduating from school. But with most boys, that is the end of it. However, the collection of autographs can be developed into a worthwhile hobby. The thing to do is to select some area of interest which appeals to you, and confine your autograph collecting to that field.

There are two basic ways to collect autographs. One is to go where the people whose signatures you want are, and struggle through the mob of admirers with your album in one hand and a pen in the other. The better way is to make a list of the names and addresses of those in the area which interests you, and write to them. If you do it in the right way, you will receive a high percentage of responses. Write a note saying that you are collecting the autographs of baseball players, or whatever it may be, and you would appreciate their signature.

Buy a packet of a hundred 3 x 5 unruled index cards, and include one with each request. Also be sure to enclose a stamped and addressed return envelope. When the signed cards come back, paste them into your autograph album; use rubber cement so that the cards can be removed in case you later wish to transfer them to a larger album, or perhaps frame and hang them up on a wall. Relate the collection to your own interests. For example, if you expect to study to be a scientist, you might collect the autographs of scientists who are famous today. Autograph collection is a very inexpensive hobby since all you need is an album, time, postage stamps, and some patience. By specializing in an interesting area, it won't take long to build up an impressive collection.

Suggested Paperback Books:

Catalogue, Walter R. Benjamin Autographs, 18 E. 77th St., New York, N.Y., free
Catalogue, Charles Hamilton Autographs, Inc., 25 E. 53rd St., New York, N.Y., free

Suggested Hard-cover Books:

Autographs: A Key to Collecting, Mary A. Benjamin (Walter R. Benjamin Autographs, 18 East 77th St., New York 21, N.Y.), $5.95, rare autographs

Indian Relics

Indian artifacts of various kinds can be found all over the United States, arrowheads being particularly plentiful. The best place to hunt for them is in a freshly plowed field after a rain. The rain washes the dirt from the stones and, by walking along the furrows, you may find an arrowhead or some other Indian relic. Though it is more fun looking for them yourself, you can also round out a collection by buying from dealers. The cost is low, a half-dozen arrowheads, for example, being obtainable for as little as a dollar.

Suggested Paperback Books:

Indian Relics and Their Values (Lightner Publishing Co.), $2.00

Indian Country, Dorothy Johnson (New York: Ballantine
     Books, Inc.), 35 cents
Indian Lore, Merit Badge Series (Boy Scouts of America),
     35 cents

Postcards and Greetings

The collection of postcards and greeting cards is a
hobby which continues in popularity throughout the
years. There are three ways to start a collection: (1)
Canvass your grandparents and other older relations and
find out if they happen to have a collection of cards that
has been put away somewhere for a long time; (2) Offer
to exchange view cards with a pen pal in some other part
of the country or abroad; (3) Buy a starter collection of
old cards from a dealer; they are inexpensive, and an interesting set of a hundred can be purchased for as little
as a dollar. Then add to your collection by getting permission to go through old stacks of social correspondence;
if you are persistent, you should eventually come up with
some real finds. You might specialize in scenic postcards,
or valentine cards, or Christmas greetings.

Suggested General Collecting Hobby Books:

Fun for Young Collectors, Joseph Leeming (Philadelphia:
     J. B. Lippincott Co.), $3.50
Old Things for Young People, Ann K. Cole (New York: David
     McKay Co., Inc.), $3.95

An excellent general reference for various collection
hobbies is the monthly periodical: *Hobbies,* The Magazine for Collectors, 1006 South Michigan Avenue, Chicago, Illinois. Your public library should have it on file.

3

"A PICTURE IS WORTH 1,000 WORDS"

THE principal advantage of visual over written expression is that the former is an international language which anyone can understand. The visual arts are much older than writing. Early man expressed himself visually with pictures drawn in sand, painted on the walls of caves, cut in bone, and with figures modeled in clay. Today we use such visual art forms as drawing, painting, sculpture, pantomime, and photography.

When you take a picture or make a sketch, you satisfy two important needs: your desire to express yourself, and your desire to communicate with others. Furthermore, your photo or drawing does not have to be translated into other languages, as a written communication would need to be. You can show it to a Frenchman, a Japanese, or a native in Somaliland. Their reactions will vary since everyone views things in a different way; but they can all see what you have done.

Many of the visual arts are used as hobbies. In addition to being fun, they provide the opportunity to develop talent you possess, of which you may be unaware. Expression through the visual arts is painlessly educational since you enjoy yourself while you are unconsciously absorbing knowledge. You also derive pleasure because you are being creative. A visual art sharpens your eyes, for you see things which a less observant viewer does not appreciate. In taking a photo of a building, for example, you begin to understand design, harmony, and beauty. Should you look at the Grand Canyon, you get a greater thrill out of it than one who has no artistic understanding. And if you take a good picture of it, you have a permanent record of an unforgettable experience.

Explore the various visual arts to find which ones light a spark in you. Photography, in particular, is so wide in its application that some one phase may well be just what you are looking for in the development of your interests and the expression of your individuality.

Fun with Photography

The most popular hobby, all over the world, for both young and old, is photography. It has universal appeal because, with a simple, inexpensive camera, anyone, without previous knowledge or training, can take reasonably good pictures and, with a bit of luck, make some excellent camera studies.

Photography is also interesting to almost everyone because the art is so flexible that it can be adapted to whatever field is desired. For example, a boy who is a sports enthusiast can specialize in action shots of athletic events. He can widen his sphere of interest as well, and, while he is carrying his camera, he can take pictures of various dramatic events.

Drama on the High Seas

One of the most famous instances of an amateur photographer being on the alert and taking highly dramatic shots happened back in 1928. On November 12 of that year, the British steamer Vestris, bound from New York City for South America, was caught in a gale off the Virginia Capes and sank, with a loss of 111 lives. Among the crew was Fred Hanson, who worked in the pantry. Just before sailing from New York, he had bought an inexpensive camera for $8.50. Shortly before the ship went down, Hanson took several snapshots of the dramatic scene. When he arrived back in New York, he showed his pictures to a reporter and, as a result, a newspaper bought and published them so that the whole story of the sinking of the ship could be shown to its readers. There are many other instances of amateur photographers who have been on their toes and taken interesting photographs that were published in newspapers or magazines.

Nature Photography

In contrast, a boy who happens to be interested in the great outdoors, the woods and fields, can put a camera to good purpose by using it to record the beauties of nature. He might specialize in scenic views of hills with unusual cloud formations above them. Or, if he lives near the sea, he can photograph the ocean in its many calm or angry moods. He can also take pictures of animals in the woods and parks, and of gulls along the shore.

Family Photography

Amateurs use their cameras most of all to photograph relatives and friends, later placing the prints in an album, thus keeping a graphic record of family life over the years. By starting to take pictures of people while you are young, you will eventually have an invaluable album of snapshots which will help you to relive many happy memories when you look through them as you grow older.

What Camera to Select

Many people are under the mistaken impression that when they are beginning as amateur photographers, the thing to do is to buy the most expensive camera they can afford. They believe this because they think that the costlier the camera, the better pictures it will take. But, as a rule, the amateur will get worse results with a high-priced camera because its mechanism is more complicated and it takes time and experimentation to learn how to use it. Therefore, in the beginning, the amateur will get more good pictures with an inexpensive box camera since its operation is very simple. A box camera has a fixed focus and only one speed. So all you have to do is to be sure that the roll is advanced to an unexposed film, look at the subject in the viewer, and snap the shutter. If you have aimed the camera properly, and there is sufficient light, most of your snaps are bound to reproduce well, though at this early stage of the game, you can't expect to get artistic results.

With an adjustable camera, on the other hand, you usually have to set the focus, the diaphragm, and the shutter speed. If any one of these is incorrect, you won't get the best results. So start off with a simple box camera. Remember, too, that film, developing, and printing cost money; and that if the pictures you take aren't good, you have wasted cash. After you have mastered the fundamentals of photography, then you can consider buying an adjustable camera. At that time you may give your first camera to someone who can learn with it as you did. Box cameras are sturdy; there are some in use today which are fifty years old, and which still take good pictures.

How to Be a Good Amateur Photographer

The basic technical factor in photography is exposure. Unless the exposure is correct, you cannot get a good picture. With a box camera, this problem is simplified as the exposures are all the same, so that all you need do is make sure that there is enough light on the subject, as explained in the instructions supplied with the camera. With adjustable cameras, the determination of the proper exposure is rather complicated, and it is advisable to purchase an exposure guide, which costs under a dollar.

The most important artistic factor in photography is composition, which is the arrangement of the subject matter within the picture area. The fundamental rule is not to have the high point of interest in the center of the shot. Observance of this rule alone will improve your photographs appreciably. There is a simple way to learn to improve your pictures pleasingly. Before snapping anything, take a small, unruled pad and draw a square or rectangle on it, depending on the shape of your picture size. Within this box, sketch in the main objects in the picture you plan to take. You don't have to be an artist, for a very simple, rough sketch will help. Do this on several sheets of paper until you have the arrangement which seems most pleasing to you. Then take your camera and move it around until you see the same composition in the view finder that you made in the sketch. This experimentation will do more to improve your pictures than anything else. Remember, composition is 90 per cent of the success in taking artistic photographs.

Candid Photography

In taking pictures of people, the amateur groups them together, tells them to say "cheese" so that they will be smiling, and then snaps the shutter. These shots frequently turn out to be pretty painful, for Mother is squinting, Dad is looking away off somewhere, Aunt Mary is frowning, and Cousin Billy is wiping his eye. To get more interesting pictures of people, do not announce that you are going to take a picture and pose the subjects. Most people freeze up when their picture is being taken and, as a result, look stiff and uncomfortable in the finished print. In candid photography, you don't ask people to pose. Instead, you snap them when they aren't looking, thereby getting lively expressions rather than frozen faces.

To take candid shots of a family gathering or other group event, put a fresh roll of film in your camera, and set it all ready to shoot. With a box camera, this is simple; with an adjustable camera, set the shutter speed at 1/50th of a second, the diaphragm at f/16, and the focus at 15 feet. Then just wander around, keeping your camera at your side or behind you so that it won't be too noticeable. Whenever you see a person or several people who are relaxed or engaged in some interesting activity, bring up your camera quickly, glance in the view finder, and snap the shutter before they know that you are taking their picture. Stay in the background, be unobtrusive, and keep your camera hidden as much as possible. After you have had a little practice, you will find that candid photography results in some of the most appealing, exciting, and often amusing, pictures you have ever taken.

The Costs of Photography

Simple box cameras cost roughly around ten dollars; adjustable cameras run anywhere from about twenty-five up to several hundred dollars. As suggested, first buy an inexpensive box camera and, if your interest in photography continues, select a more expensive camera later on. Then there is the cost of film and the charge for developing and printing, which, for black-and-white pictures, is around a dollar a roll. Processing color pictures costs three to four times as much. It is not recommended that you go in for color photography until you have sufficient photographic experience and can afford the extra costs. Keep in mind that it is much better to make excellent black-and-white pictures than poor color photographs. Though you can save money by developing and printing your own pictures, it takes a lot of practice to get good results and is not advisable unless you have an interest in chemistry, or are just naturally curious about the developing process and would like to see it in action.

Photography, as millions have learned, is fun. If you are the outdoor type, it can add to the pleasure of your activities by recording them permanently. Or if you would like to take indoor pictures, you can experiment with flashlight photography. Whatever type of pictures you prefer to take, you will derive great enjoyment out of shooting with a camera and, too, you will also gain an appreciation of composition, orderliness, and beauty that will serve to enrich your life.

Suggested Paperback Books:

Kodak Camera Guide (New York: Pocket Books, Inc.), 50
    cents

How to Make Good Pictures, Eastman Kodak Company,
    Rochester, New York, $1.00

Making Your Picture Interesting, Little Technical Library
    (New York: Crown Publishers, Inc.), $1.00

1,000 Answers to Questions About Photography, Robert L.
    McIntyre (New York: Grosset & Dunlap, Inc.), $1.95

Photography, No. 3334, Merit Badge Library (Boy Scouts of
    America), 35 cents

Suggested Hard-cover Books:

Boys' Book of Photography, Edwin Way Teale (New York:
    E. P. Dutton & Co.), $3.75

First Book of Photography, John Hoke (New York: Franklin
    Watts, Inc.), $2.50

Sketching and Cartooning

In attempting any art form, the first thing is to find out
if you are talented in that particular direction. Should
you find that you have no talent whatever, then that's
that. But if you discover that you do have some talent,
however little, you should explore its possibilities.

Learning to Draw

Sketching, which is simplest, and costs little for supplies, should be investigated first. All you need is a soft
pencil and an unruled pad. Begin by copying simple illu-

strations from newspapers and magazines. Let us say you copy a sketch of a cat. Draw it several times, trying to improve as you go along. Then put away the original drawing and try to sketch the cat from memory. An artist must be able to picture things vividly in his mind's eye. If you can draw an object without having it before you, it shows that you have a good memory and an active imagination.

Up to this point, you have been copying and visualizing. Now draw the cat—or whatever subject you have selected—and make the sketch with as few pencil lines as possible. In this way, you will be experimenting and developing an original style.

Very likely you will soon turn to sketching other subjects, whatever your fancy may be. However, you can keep on drawing the same thing all the time. Many artists specialize, drawing or painting just cats, dogs, horses, or whatever, thereby gaining a reputation for their skill in depicting a certain subject in various ways.

Improving Your Talent

If your talent is modest, you can continue to enjoy sketching as an interesting and pleasant hobby. However, should you find that you improve with practice, then you might consider taking up the more difficult art medium of painting with watercolors or oils. Don't try "painting by the numbers" as it is so oversimplified a method that it is of no value whatever in the improvement of your talent and technique. Instead, get a small painting kit for around ten dollars or so, and buy a book of instructions or borrow it from your public library. From then on, the development of your talent is up to you.

Cartooning

Your talent for sketching may be minor, but you can still get a lot of fun out of it by testing your skill at drawing cartoons. Study the techniques used in the comic strips in the newspapers and the cartoons in various magazines, and you will find that many are very simply drawn. Select one you like and copy several of the strips in pencil to get your hand in. Then take a strip and, using your imagination, draw the figures in your own way in order to develop originality.

Now try doing some single-panel cartoons, which consist of a drawing and a short gag line underneath. First, you have to dream up some funny gags. Let's say, for example, you show a couple of Boy Scouts trying to start a fire by friction and obviously getting nowhere. The gag line could be "Got a match?"

The best way to practice gag writing is to go through the cartoons in the magazines and rewrite the gags, trying to make them as good as, or perhaps even funnier than, the ones that were printed. For instance, the gag for the Boy Scout cartoon could be changed to "Let's pray for lightning."

Once you have progressed to the point where you can draw reasonably well with a style of your own, start working with black ink on heavier paper, obtainable in pads at any art supply store. When you have about a dozen sketches or cartoons you like, put them up on the walls of your room, using rubber cement so that they will be readily removable. Change your informal art exhibit now and then, putting up new ones and pasting the old ones in a scrapbook. Perhaps your parents will suggest that you display your best drawings in the family recreation room; or you may belong to a club where they can be shown "on loan," as artists say.

Drawing and painting, like photography, develop artistic appreciation. With it, you will select things not only for their useful value, but also because of the pleasing way in which they are designed. An eye for harmony and decorative value will add much to the pleasures of living throughout the years.

Suggested Paperback Books:

How to Draw the Human Figure, John Grabach (New York: Dell Books), 50 cents

It's Fun to Draw, A. D. Bogorad (New York: Tudor Publishing Co.), $1.45

Junior's Fun to Draw, A. D. Bogorad, ed. (New York: Tudor Publishing Co.), $1.45

Art, No. 3320, Merit Badge Library (Boy Scouts of America), 35 cents

Cartooning, Jean Arestein (New York: Sterling Publishing Co., Inc.), $1.00

Suggested Hard-cover Books:

First Book of Drawing, Louis Slobodkin (New York: Franklin Watts, Inc.), $2.50

How to Draw Landscapes, Seascapes and Cityscapes, Arthur Zaidenberg (New York: Abelard-Schuman, Ltd.), $3.00

How to Draw Ships and Trains, Cars and Airplanes, Arthur Zaidenberg (New York: Abelard-Schuman, Ltd.), $3.00

How to Draw Cartoons, A. Zaidenberg (New York: Vanguard Press, Inc.), $3.00

Sketching and Painting Indoors, Adrian Hill (New York: Pit-
man Publishing Corp.), $2.75
Sketching and Painting Out of Doors, Adrian Hill (New York:
Pitman Publishing Corp.), $2.75

Related Visual Hobbies

Since "a picture is worth 1,000 words," it follows that
the same must hold true for all other forms of visual art,
whether they be sculpture, mobiles, or anything else. You
can prove this by performing an interesting experiment.
Look over your snapshots and select a busy street scene,
or perhaps a shot taken at a baseball or football game.
The actual camera work took you only a minute or so,
maybe even less. Now with the print before you, take a
pad of ruled paper and try to describe the entire scene in
words. It may require a few hundred or even over a thousand, and you will find it difficult, very likely impossible, to
describe the whole picture in every detail. You can use a
snapshot of a building or of a statue in a park, and the
results will invariably be the same. The visual arts are
highly effective, both artistically and emotionally, because
they have dramatic impact.

Movie Photography

Shooting movies is a far cry from taking still pictures.
However, movie cameras, inexpensively priced, are available today which any amateur can readily learn to use
with good results. Taking color movies is also possible
by anyone. In addition, sound can be synchronized with
film, if desired, though naturally the adding of extra
equipment makes it more costly.

Suggested Paperback Books:

Kodak Home Movie Camera Guide (New York: Pocket Books, Inc.), 50 cents

How to Switch from Still Photography to Moviemaking, E. A. Gilmour (New York: A. S. Barnes & Co.), 95 cents

Color Movies for the Beginner, Harris B. Tuttle, Little Technical Library (New York: Crown Publishers, Inc.), $1.00

Suggested Hard-cover Books:

How to Take Better Home Movies, Peter Gowland (New York: Arco Publishing Co., Inc.), $2.50

Color Transparencies

You can take color transparencies with any 35-mm camera and eventually build up an interesting library of pictures. The particular advantage of color transparencies is that they can be seen in all their brilliance with a viewer, and they can also be projected on a wall or screen to many times their original size. You can also get transparencies without having a camera by purchasing them in camera shops and elsewhere, where they are available in a large variety of subjects. Reels of three-dimensional color transparencies, which require a special, inexpensive viewer, are also obtainable; just ask your dealer for a free list of View-master picture reels.

Sculpture

Curiously enough, men whittle at two periods in their lives: when they are young, and again when they are old.

Most do nothing more than whittle idly on a stick; but, if you find that you have "a feel for wood," perhaps you should try making objects and figures out of wood. There are many other media you can use for carving or sculpturing. Clay is a good medium since it is easily shaped with the fingers. Stone, being hard, is naturally much more difficult to sculpt, and perhaps should be left to those talented in that direction.

Suggested Paperback Books:

Sculpture, No. 3322, Merit Badge Library (Boy Scouts of America), 35 cents

Woodcarving, No. 3315, Merit Badge Library (Boy Scouts of America), 35 cents

Tips on Soap Carving, National Soap Sculpture Committee, Box 202 Church Street Station, New York, N.Y., free

Suggested Hard-cover Books:

Anyone Can Sculpt, Arthur Zaidenberg (New York: Harper & Row, Publishers), $4.50

Clay, Wood, and Wire, Harvey Weiss (New York: William R. Scott, Inc.), $3.75

Painting

Painting is more difficult than sketching; nevertheless, the number of amateur painters, both young and old, runs into the millions. Should you try painting with watercolors or in oils, you'll want to wear old clothes since things are inclined to get rather messy around your easel.

Suggested Paperback Books:

It's Fun to Paint, Arnold Blanch and Doris Lee (New York: Tudor Publishing Co.), $1.45

Painting as a Pastime, Winston S. Churchill (New York: Cornerstone Library, Inc.), $1.00

Suggested Hard-cover Books:

Beginner's Book of Oil Painting, Adrian Hill (New York: Emerson Books, Inc.), $2.95

Painting for Children, Marjorie Rentoul (Los Angeles: Bob Spencer Book Company), $4.50

4

LET'S COMMUNICATE

MAN's most common form of communication is oral. In addition, through the ages, he has developed sign language, hieroglyphics, and written language as we know it today. One of man's most useful tools is writing. It expresses ideas, and it is permanent. It can take the form of poetry, like Shakespeare's, or a memorable speech, like Lincoln's Gettysburg Address. It may be a lively letter to a friend, or a clearly understandable business communication.

"It is easy to be a writer," William Jackson Lord, Ph.D., has said. "All one needs is paper and stamps. There is no license, no defined education, no apprenticeship required. One just sails in and writes."

Whatever your adult interests may turn out to be, facility in writing can be of great help to you in your business and social contacts. Meanwhile, you can get much pleasure and enjoyment from using communication as a hobby in either oral or written form. Remember that all hobbies are educational, to a greater or lesser degree, depending upon their nature; but that is not your purpose in taking them up. Communication is highly educational and of great value in life because if you cannot communicate with others, you might as well be a hermit on a hill, talking to yourself while you are twiddling your thumbs.

Communication is a two-way street: you should be able to communicate clearly with people, and you should understand them when they communicate with you. It has been found that students who read easily and understandably are able to absorb knowledge much faster than those who cannot. In recent years, reading machines have been developed which are very effective in improving the retention of knowledge from the written word. If you have any difficulty in reading, ask about these special courses at your school.

Is some aspect of written communication an appropriate hobby for you? If you get good grades in English, grammar, and composition, very likely you have some talent for writing which can be developed. However, if you don't shine in this area, it doesn't necessarily follow that you should skip communication. In fact, it's all the more reason you should explore the field because, while you are making it a pleasurable pastime, you will also improve your grades at school.

Picking a Pen Pal

A good way to start improving your writing ability is by corresponding with a pen pal. Various magazines print letters from persons who are seeking correspondents. In choosing one to write to, you might select a boy who lives in another country who can write in English. You can exchange picture postcards—eventually building up a colorful collection—and, in your letters, you can describe the various customs in your respective homelands. If you are studying a foreign language, you may want to correspond with someone who can write that language as well.

You may also like to correspond with a relative who resides in some other part of your own country. Ask your Dad and Mother if there isn't some cousin, a boy around your own age, to whom you might write and ask if he would like to carry on a casual correspondence. When your pen pal is a relative, it is likely that your acquaintance may grow to the point where you eventually meet each other, either at his home or at yours. Lifetime friendships have developed from correspondence with a pen pal. And the writing of such letters, though informal, serves to improve your writing style.

The advantage of writing to a pen pal is that you don't have to be concerned with rules of composition. Such a correspondence should not be a chore; for, if it is, then its basic purpose, which is enjoyment, is defeated, and it is no longer a hobby. Keep in mind that a hobby must be fun. There is a "trick" in social correspondence that makes it a pleasure rather than an obligation. The idea is to forget formality and write much as you talk. Something along these lines:

Hi, Dick:

Thanks a lot for your last letter. I got a charge out of your description of the picnic your family had on the edge of the Grand Canyon. But it's not for me, pal. I get dizzy when I'm way up somewhere. It's called—wait until I look it up in the dictionary—acrophobia, meaning fear of high places. So if you're ever around this way, I'll take you on a picnic down in a cave. That's for me! . . .

If you've never won a spelling bee—or even if you have—keep a dictionary handy. Though you write as casually as you converse with a friend, there is no excuse for sloppy spelling. With that single exception, forget the formalities, and just let the words flow. After a while, you will find that your thoughts pour out faster than you can write them down. This naturally leads us to a handy aid which is in common use, even in the home, today.

Tickling a Typewriter

If you decide to go in for written communication as a hobby, once you get rolling, you should consider the use of a typewriter. Maybe there is already one in your home which you can get permission to operate. If not, an old, battered machine that still behaves reasonably well, can be purchased for from ten dollars up to twenty-five or so. And if you really go for this hobby, perhaps your parents can help you to get one of the new portable machines. Whether your typewriter is secondhand or new, it is a good idea to learn to type by the touch system. Many reporters and rewrite men on newspapers, and even professional writers, type with three fingers. However, use of the touch system increases speed and reduces the number of errors. A typing chart costs only a dollar or so, and with a half-hour of daily practice, you can type fairly accurately and rapidly within a month, with your skill gradually improving thereafter. In later life, whatever your vocation may be, you will find that being able to type can be put to good use in your work and also at home.

Suggested Paperback Books:

Typing Made Simple, Nathan Levine, Made Simple Books
(Garden City, N.Y.: Doubleday & Co., Inc.), $1.45
Typing for Your Needs, Marion J. Russell and Donald A.
Boyer (Pittsburgh, Pa.: Boxwood Press), $2.15

Doodling with a Diary

At first thought, you might feel that keeping a diary is
more appropriate for members of the opposite sex, since
they are supposed to be more talkative than men. But
once you listen to a group of males at a club meeting, or
hear legislators argue for hours about some disputed bill,
you may well logically conclude that we are as wordy as
the women, if not even more so. In any case, the most
famous—and the longest!—diary ever published was written by an Englishman, Samuel Pepys, who devised a
shorthand system of his own to record in great detail the
day-to-day events in his life for ten years (1660-1669).
Though he held high offices in government service, he
would be unknown to the world today were it not for his
classic diary. Thus, we see that even as simple a thing as
a diary can become deathless literature.

Keeping a diary is not a major hobby, but it can be of
value to every hobbyist, whatever his interests may be.
Many people feel that they are much too busy to keep a
daily diary. Actually the person who maintains a well-
ordered life is never too busy to take time for something
worthwhile. However, writing in a diary is easy and takes
little time if, instead of doing it every day, you set aside
fifteen minutes or so once a week to jot down the interest-

ing events of the past seven days. They need be only short notes sufficient to remind you of particular occasions; your memory will supply you with the rest of the details.

If you like, you may use your diary as a place to write down the various riddles and rhymes, jokes and funny stories, clever sayings and tongue twisters, that you hear from time to time. Then you will have them all in one place for handy reference when you want to repeat them to someone else.

A diary is of value in checking "what happened when." Jot down briefly the interesting points of a Boy Scout hike or a club meeting; keep a record of birthdays, anniversaries, holidays, and graduations; note when you started a hobby, and how you progressed. In later years, you will enjoy glancing through it and reliving your younger days, some of which you may otherwise have forgotten. In a diary, you are communicating with yourself. And who could have a better friend?

Suggested Paperback Books:

Diary of a Civil War Hero, Michael Dougherty (New York: Pyramid Books), 50 cents
Diary of a Young Girl, Anne Frank (New York: Pocket Books, Inc.), 35 cents
Diary of Samuel Pepys (abridged) O. F. Morshead, ed. (New York: Harper & Row, Publishers, Torchbooks), $2.45

The Craft of Creative Writing

Of all the free-lance authors who write short stories or novels, articles or nonfiction books, over ninety per cent do so on a part-time basis, deriving the major portion of their income from some other source. Creative writing, therefore, is an avocation or hobby for most people; and it attracts millions because it is an intensely personal and highly creative art form.

If you have any talent at all for writing, however little, it can be developed into a fascinating hobby. Writing letters and keeping a diary help to develop an interesting literary style. Then you can experiment with the writing of short articles, which is much simpler than learning the technique of writing fiction. Flip through your diary, select an interesting experience, and write it up briefly. Then give it a colorful title. Don't call it, "A Day in the Country," which is dull; rather title it something like, "Fishing for Trout in the Berkshires," or whatever is appropriate.

All creative writers like to see their work in print. So when you have completed an article, correct any errors in spelling, punctuation, and grammar, and then type it, making a carbon copy for your own file. In preparing material for possible publication, note that it has to be neatly typewritten, for handwritten manuscripts are not considered. It must be double-spaced, too. Put your name and address in the upper lefthand corner, and the approximate number of words in the upper righthand corner. Attach a self-addressed, stamped envelope for the return of the article to you, in case it is rejected. Then submit it to some publication you know of, a club or church school paper, some other periodical which circulates in your community, perhaps your local newspaper. Address it to the editor, and be sure to put sufficient postage on both envelopes.

Very likely your article will be returned to you with regret. But there is always the possibility, however slender, that an editor will like it well enough to publish it. Don't be discouraged if you find that you are collecting rejection slips; professional writers often get them. When the article comes back from one publication, immediately mail it to another. Meanwhile, write several more articles and, when they are as good as you can possibly make them, send them out on their publishers' rounds, too.

In taking up writing, remember that you are not trying to write for money—many small publications do not pay for unsolicited contributions. You are doing it as a pleasurable hobby to increase whatever degree of creative writing talent you may possess. And if you should have something published, you will get a thrill out of seeing it in print under your name, even though you are not paid for it. Relatives and friends will see your article and congratulate you, and you will be a neighborhood celebrity, a "seven-day wonder." But don't rest on your laurels. After you have had one piece published, you will be eager to write more; you may even try fiction. And in time your hobby may develop into a very pleasant—perhaps even modestly profitable—pastime.

Suggested Paperback Books:

The Art of Writing Made Simple, Irving Rosenthal and Morton Yarmon, Made Simple Books (Garden City, N.Y.: Doubleday & Co., Inc.), $1.45

Key to a Better Vocabulary, Hal G. Vermes (New York: Key Books), $1.00

Word Mastery Made Simple, Arthur Waldhorn and Arthur

Zeiger, Made Simple Books (Garden City, N.Y.: Doubleday & Co., Inc.), $1.45

Writing Fiction, R. V. Cassill (New York: Pocket Books),
75 cents

U. S. Government Printing Office *Style Manual,* Government
Printing Office, Washington, D.C. 20402, $1.25

Suggested Hard-cover Books:

Writing as a Career, Norman Lobsenz (New York: Henry Z.
Walck, Inc.), $3.50

Someday You'll Write, Elizabeth Yates (New York: E. P.
Dutton & Co.), $2.75

Communicating by Tape Recorder

There is an interesting new method of communication
which is just coming into general use. Instead of writing
letters in social correspondence, some people dictate letters on tape to relatives and friends. If you have never
received a taped letter, you will be surprised and thrilled
when you hear the voice of a relative or friend through
the loud speaker of a tape recorder. Perhaps it is someone
living far away whom you haven't met and whose voice
you haven't heard on the telephone. After you have listened to the taped letter—very likely you will play it
over several times—you can reply in the same way and
your correspondent will then hear your voice for the first
time. If you would like to take up this new hobby of
communication by tape, here is how to go about it.

First, you must, of course, purchase a tape recorder,
but it is not so costly as you might think. In fact, battery-

operated, transistorized portable tape recorders can be purchased for around ten dollars, and sometimes even less. Other machines run over a hundred dollars, but you don't need an expensive one for this purpose. The reels of tape cost about seventy-five cents, the price depending on the quality and length of the magnetized tape. Some reels record for twenty minutes; others have a capacity of up to two hours. You don't have to keep buying new reels since they can be used over and over—the previous recording is automatically erased when you dictate on the tape again—and the reels last for years. You need only as many reels as you have correspondents because, when you send them a taped letter, after they have listened to it, they reply on the same tape and mail it back to you. Since the reels of tape weigh only two or three ounces, the cost of postage is very little. So you can start the modern hobby of communication by tape with a total investment of ten dollars or so.

Before you mail a letter by tape to anyone, send postcards to relatives and friends who live out of town and ask them if they have a tape recorder. There should be several so equipped since tape recording is rapidly becoming a popular hobby, and as time goes by more people you know will have recorders. Now turn on your machine, press the dictating button, pick up the microphone, and start "writing" your first "talkie" letter. You'll find it great fun and, too, as you learn to speak into the "mike" with ease and informality, you will painlessly improve your style of oral communication.

A tape recorder can also be used for other purposes. You can dictate your diary on a tape once a week instead of writing it. If you have a talk to give at school or elsewhere, you can practice it on the tape recorder, listen to it, and repeat it several times on the same tape until you have it down pat. Many professional singers and musicians record their voices or instruments on tape while practicing their solos. Thus if you are musically inclined, you can use your machine for that purpose, too. There is a story about a certain bashful young man in his twenties, who was too shy to ask his sweetheart's hand in marriage. So he dictated his proposal on tape, doing it over and over until it was letter perfect, and then he mailed it to her. As the tale goes, it was so dramatic and convincing that she accepted him and they lived happily ever after. Whether or not you one day propose to the love of your life in that manner, you are certain to get a lot of enjoyment out of the hobby of tape recording.

Suggested Paperback Books:

Tape Recorders—How They Work, Charles G. Westcott (Indianapolis, Ind.: Bobbs-Merrill Co., Inc.), $2.75

ABC's of Tape Recording, Norman Crowhurst (Indianapolis, Ind.: Bobbs-Merrill Co., Inc.), $1.50

Suggested Hard-cover Books:

Tape Recording as a Pastime, Ian Arnison and Douglas Gardner (New York: Taplinger Publishing Co., Inc.), $3.00

Communicating Around the World

There is a thrilling way of reaching countries around the world which few people in the United States know about, though it is quite popular in other places all over the globe. It is by means of short-wave radio. With a radio of this type, you can tune in the programs of hundreds of stations, thousands of miles away. Even the least expensive set, with a good outdoor aerial, can pull in signals from the most distant points.

The fun of "DXing," as it is called, is in making a record of the stations you hear, and then writing them for confirmation. When you log a station anywhere in the world, make a note of its call letters, the city and country of origin, the time of day, and the type of program you heard. Most foreign stations broadcast programs regularly in English. Send this information to the station, tell them how well their signal was received, and request a verification. Enclose an International Reply Coupon for return postage; obtainable from any post office for fifteen cents each. Be sure to put the right amount of postage on your letter. In return, you will receive a verification, which is usually in the form of a postcard that is beautifully printed in color. And, of course, there will be a cancelled foreign stamp on the card. These QSL cards, as they are called, make a most unusual and colorful collection, when they are put into an album, which you will be proud to show to your family and friends.

DXing on the short-wave bands is an excellent pastime, particularly on long winter evenings, which is usually the time when signals come in best. Short-wave reception is affected by sunspots and other meteorological conditions. Some days the signals from stations halfway around the world will come in strongly on your earphones; at other times even the programs from nearby stations will be heard only faintly. So you have to keep at it to bring in stations five or ten thousand miles away. But, if you are persistent, you will eventually have an impressive list of stations which you have logged around the globe, and an album of distinctive verification cards.

Short-wave receivers cost from around fifty dollars up to well over a hundred. As has been mentioned, even the simpler sets can, with a good aerial, log stations all over the world. If you are handy with tools, and know how to handle electrical circuits safely, you can buy a kit and make your own short-wave receiver for about twenty dollars.

Suggested Paperback Books:

ABC's of Short-Wave Listening, Len Buckwalter (Indianapolis, Ind.: Bobbs-Merrill Co., Inc.), $1.95

World Radio TV Handbook, O. Lund Johansen, Ltd., Lindorffsalle 1, Hellerup, Denmark, $3.00 (also available at some radio supply stores)

Radio, Merit Badge Series (Boy Scouts of America), 35 cents

Amazing World of Short Wave Listening, Hallicrafters Co., Dept. 34, Chicago, Illinois, free booklet

Suggested Hard-cover Books:

Boys' Book of Communications, Raymond F. Yates (New York: Harper & Row, Publishers), $2.75

Two-Way Radio Communication

With a short-wave receiving set, the communication is only one way: from the radio stations to you. The natural next step, if radio interests you as a hobby, is to become a "ham operator," as you would be called, and have your own amateur radio station. Then you will be able to communicate with other hams, either by International Morse Code or voice. This is an extremely popular hobby as evidenced by the fact that there are well over a quarter-million licensed amateur radio stations in the United States, many of them manned by boys.

If you have a short-wave receiver, you can determine how ham radio would appeal to you by tuning in on the amateur bands and listening to the operators chatting back and forth all over the country and the world. There is no privacy in radio and anyone can listen in.

There are just three basic parts needed for an amateur radio station: receiver, transmitter, and power unit. Should you already have a receiver, you add the other two. The cost, if you buy kits and assemble them, runs from fifty dollars up.

Besides their enjoying a fascinating hobby, amateur radio operators have proved to be of great value in times of emergency. When, for example, there is a flood and all other means of communication are washed out, ham operators work with government agencies and the Red Cross in sending out calls for assistance and transmitting messages covering relief operations. If you have a little technical skill, and can learn to read diagrams, you should give serious consideration to taking up this absorbing and enjoyable hobby.

Suggested Paperback Books:

Amateur Radio Station Manual (Indianapolis, Ind.: Howard W. Sams & Co., Inc.), $3.95

Amateur Radio Construction Projects, Charles Caringella (Indianapolis: Howard W. Sams & Co., Inc.), $2.50

Federal Communications Commission Rules and Regulations, Government Printing Office, Washington, D.C. 20402, 30 cents

Ham Radio for the Whole Family, free
Learning the Radiotelegraph Code, 50 cents
How to Become a Radio Amateur, 50 cents   American Radio Relay League, West Hartford, Conn.
Operating an Amateur Radio Station, 25 cents
Radio Amateur's License Manual, 50 cents

Radio Builder's Handbook, 25 cents   Allied Radio Corp., 100 North Western Ave., Chicago, Illinois
Radio Circuit Handbook, 25 cents

Communicating by Music

Music is a hobby that is growing in popularity. Twice as many Americans play musical instruments today as they did twenty-five years ago. Music communicates your feelings, whether they are sad, happy, tender, or aggressive. For the talented, there are the piano and violin. Those who just want to fool around with music can take up a simpler instrument like the recorder, guitar, ukulele, banjo, harmonica, or xylophone. Your own voice is another instrument right at hand that costs nothing, unless you want to have it trained. For ordinary purposes, if you can read music, you can have fun by joining a chorus or choir, or a folk music group.

Suggested Paperback Books:

Folksinger's Guitar Guide, Pete Seeger and Jerry Silverman (New York: Oak Publications), $2.95

How to Make Music on the Harmonica, P. V. Planta (New York: Sentinel Books Publ., Inc.), $1.00

How to Play 5-String Banjo, Pete Seeger (New York: Oak Publications), $2.00

Let's Play the Recorder, Robert Bouchard (Boston: Bruce Humphries, Pubs.), $2.00

How to Play the Harmonica, Sigmund Spaeth, M. Hohner, Inc., Andrews Road, Hicksville, Long Island, N.Y., free booklet

Folksongs for Fun, Oscar Brand, ed. (New York: Berkley Books), 60 cents

Suggested Hard-cover Books:

America Sings, Carl Carmer (New York: Alfred A. Knopf, Inc.), $5.99

Learning Music, Lena Milam (Austin, Tex.: Steck Co.), 76 cents

5

LET'S EXPLORE NATURE

MOUNTAINEERS say they climb mountains just because the mountains are there. It is much the same with nature: we can all enjoy it simply because it is there. Even the city dweller has parks to roam in; and it usually takes only a short ride on a bicycle or bus to get out into the country. In addition, there is the opportunity to have fun in natural surroundings when one is at summer camp or on vacation elsewhere. Besides, adventuring in the great outdoors is healthful, as your family doctor will confirm.

Most males are natural outdoorsmen, an inclination bred into them by ancestors who cut homesteads out of the wilderness, built cabins, fashioned boats, fished and hunted for food. If you feel "the call of the wild," you don't have to be urged to get out in the sun, the storm, and the snow. If you are a homebody, that is all the more reason why you should explore the woods and hills, the brooks and ponds in your locality. Though you don't have to understand nature to derive pleasure from it, the more you know about it, the greater your enjoyment will be.

Nature hobbies are normally inexpensive since much is provided without cost from nature's endless supply. In fishing, you have to supply the pole and bait, but nature provides the fish. In collecting rocks and other minerals, you can bang away with a geologist's hammer for a lifetime and hardly make a dent in the earth's crust. In the study of insects, you will find so many everywhere that you'll hardly know where to begin.

Hobbies in the field of nature are simple to take up, low in cost, healthful, and enjoyable; and they can be indulged in by anyone, anywhere in the world. They are particularly fascinating because the variety and supply are so great that the nature hobbyist—however long he has been at it—is always making new discoveries. If you will consider the following selection of nature hobbies you will be very likely to find at least one that can provide you with endless hours of pleasure.

Going Fishing

"Catching fish is not the whole of fishing," an old proverb reminds us. There's the joyful feeling of complete freedom that you cannot have in the confines of city or town. There's the excitement of a sudden strike and playing the fish into the net. There's the companionship of other fishermen and the tall tales told around the campfire. There's the pan-fried brook trout, which tastes so much better than the frozen fish bought at a supermarket. And finally, there is the opportunity to think and dream in solitude. The full title of the classic book on fishing, written by Izaak Walton over three centuries ago, is *The Compleat Angler, or the Contemplative Man's Recreation.*"

A fisherman never gets bored with fishing, because there are always new places to fish, in the oceans, lakes, and streams that cover two-thirds of the earth's surface.

There are two dozen fresh water species to choose from and over 200 salt water fish you can try to catch. Fishing is one of the most popular sports, there being twenty-five million licensed anglers, eighteen million of them boys and men, seven million women. Though fishermen spend a shade over a hundred dollars a year on this sport, many a fish has been caught by a boy with a pole cut from a tree, some store string, a bent pin, and a worm. So whatever your equipment may be, speak to your dad or a friend and say, "Let's go fishing!"

Suggested Paperback Books:

Fishing, George Fichter, Merit Badge Series (Boy Scouts of America), 35 cents

The Fundamentals of Fishing and Hunting, Byron Dalrymple (New York: Pocket Books, Inc.), 35 cents

Fishing for Boys, Tom McNally (Chicago: Follett Publishing Co.), $1.00

Fisherman's Handbook, Rube Allyn (Great Outdoors Publishing Co.), 65 cents

Secrets of Successful Fishing, Henry Shakespeare, Shakespeare Co., Kalamazoo, Mich. 49002, 50 cents in coins.

Suggested Hard-cover Books:

Young Sportsman's Guide to Fresh Water Fishing, Ray Ovington (Camden, N.J.: Nelson-National), $2.75

Fishing, Wm. Moore (New York: G. P. Putnam's Sons), $2.95

Let's Fish, Harry Zarchy (New York: Alfred A. Knopf, Inc.), $3.75

Life in a Fishbowl

Living in a glass house doesn't appeal to us human beings because we'd have no privacy. However, fish in an aquarium—though subject to nervous diseases—do not seem to mind it. And since we can observe their actions at all times, having an aquarium of lively, colorful fish is a hobby whose fascination never diminishes. Attesting to its leadership is the fact that aquarium fish are by far the most popular of all pets in the American home, being enjoyed by twenty million families.

Practically everyone, when he was young, has had a goldfish or two in a small bowl of water, acquired for thirty-nine cents or so, which soon died from lack of proper care. It is a far cry from that simple pastime to a tank stocked with several beautiful varieties of tropical fish selected from among the hundreds available at pet shops today.

Being an aquarist is an excellent extra hobby since it takes little time, and a tank filled with colorful tropicals is very decorative. The cost is reasonable, being from ten dollars up, though later on, you can, if your interest continues, spend fifty dollars and up for a larger tank, providing room for more fish, and a pump and an aerator.

As with any other hobby, start off modestly, spending little, until you are assured that you really want to pursue this hobby. A five-gallon tank is big enough for a beginning, and one that is rectangular in shape is to be preferred as you can set it on a window sill where the fish can get natural light. You can also give them additional light with a two-bulb reflector. Place a piece of glass on top of the tank, leaving about an inch of air space along the back. Put the reflector above the glass cover. Spread about a half-inch of gravel, purchased at a pet shop, over the bottom of the tank. Then landscape the aquarium with several plants which, when stuck in the gravel, will usually grow so fast that you have to trim them down occasionally. Age fresh, clean water for twelve hours before pouring it slowly into the tank. Later, when adding water because of natural evaporation, use a thermometer to make certain that the new water is approximately the same temperature as that already in the tank.

One of the two most common causes of failure is over-crowding of fish. A rough rule of thumb is to have no more than two fish per gallon. However, if you add an air pump, aerator, and filter, usually costing under ten dollars, you can double the number of fish. In addition, you should have a glass dip tube for cleaning dirt from the bottom of the tank, and a dip net for removing fish when necessary.

In a five-gallon tank, you can have ten fish without aeration, and twenty with it. For colorful variety, buy tropical fish in pairs. If some of them are live-bearers, such as guppies, platys, and black mollies, and the pairs turn out to be male and female, one day you will be surprised to discover a dozen or more offspring, not much larger than a pinhead, dashing about the tank and hiding among the plants. Search them out with a dip net and put them, along with water from the tank, in a small glass bowl for a while; otherwise, their parents may eat them!

The second common cause of failure is overfeeding. Food that is not consumed will foul the water and eventually kill off the fish. So give them only as much food as they can consume within five minutes, and feed them twice a day, if possible; if you can feed them only once a day, make it in the morning. If you are away for a couple of days, don't worry, for the fish can get along without food for several days without starving. In fact, if you go on a two-week vacation once a year, they will still survive.

In becoming an aquarist as a hobby, start with goldfish, which are more sturdy, and then progress to tropicals, varying the species as others die off. Later add the pump, aerator, and filter so that you can double the number of fish. Begin with a five-gallon tank, and get larger sizes if your interest continues. In breeding fish, stick to livebearers because they don't require any extra attention except in protecting the babies from their cannibalistic parents. The breeding of egg bearers is complicated, so wait until you are an experienced aquarist before attempting it. Meanwhile, you can learn a lot about tropical fish, and have fun while observing their private lives through the walls of their glass home.

Suggested Paperback Books:

A Guide to Tropical Fish, Nathan H. and Sylvia K. Mager (New York: Washington Square Press), 60 cents

Pets, Merit Badge Series (Boy Scouts of America), 35 cents

The Complete Book of Pet Care, Howard J. Lewis, Maco Magazine Corp., 75 cents

Aquariums, Anthony Evans (New York: Dover Publications, Inc.), 75 cents

Suggested Hard-cover Books:

How to Keep and Breed Tropical Fish, C. W. Emmens (New York: Sterling Publishing Co., Inc.), $4.95

Playing with a Parakeet

Having pets, whether they be tropical fish, dogs, cats, canaries, or parakeets, is a secondary hobby, unless one breeds and raises them professionally, when it becomes a vocation. There is no need to go into the selection and care of such popular pets as dogs, cats, and canaries since practically everyone has had one or more, and thus has at least some basic knowledge about them. The parakeet, however, deserves special mention since only in recent years has this native of Australia become popular in the United States, and because, though it is a small bird, weighing hardly an ounce, it is very lively, and can be easily trained to talk and do tricks, as well.

The scientific name for this colorful bird is "budgerigar," but since it is rather difficult to pronounce, they are popularly called "parakeets," "budgies," or simply, "keets." If you have never had a budgie, you are in for a treat, some surprises, and a lot of laughs, because these playful birds almost seem to have a sense of humor. As Howard J. Lewis (see his book on pet care listed below) amusingly puts it, they have an "amiable attitude toward higher education."

The parakeet, though related to the parrot, is much smaller—a distinct advantage in the selection of a bird pet. The larger birds, such as the parrot, the cockateel, and the lovebird, are strong enough to inflict a bite with their beaks which really hurts, and may be severe enough to draw blood. But when the little keet affectionately nibbles on a finger or ear, the bite doesn't hurt and causes no injury. Also to be considered is the fact that small birds naturally have small droppings. In the case of the budgie, if it is well its droppings become dry almost immediately and can be brushed away like powder without leaving a stain on furniture or clothing.

Buy your budgie at a good pet shop where you can rely on getting a healthy, lively bird of the right age. Ask for a keet that is between one and two months as older birds are more difficult to train. Parakeets cost from under two dollars up to around five dollars, depending on the color markings of the feathers. A male has a blue band (cere) at the top of the beak, while the female's is tan or brown. But the sex of a budgie doesn't really matter, for both make good pets. You will need a cage, too, of course, which sells from three dollars or so up to twenty-five and more, depending on size and construction. Because a parakeet is a small bird, it doesn't need a large cage, especially since, after it has been trained, you can let it stay out of the cage much of the time. It is an intensely curious creature and loves to investigate everything in the room where it is kept. Some people give a keet the run of the house, but this is unsafe, for it may dart out of a window or door—in which case it will surely get lost since it has no means of finding its way back home. So keep your budgie in one room, and place the cage where it will be out of any drafts. More parakeets die from catching a cold than from any other reason.

Teaching a parakeet to talk is loads of fun, though it does take patience and persistence. While you hold your pupil on a forefinger or a stick, repeat a word over and over for about five minutes, and continue the lesson each day until he has learned to say it without prompting. "Hello" and "goodby" might be the first two words. Speak clearly but not loudly as it is easily frightened, especially until it feels at home in your company. After the keet has learned "hello," add a word to it, saying, "Hello, baby"; and when it has learned that phrase, add two or three more words—for example, "Hello, baby, how are you?" A budgie can learn a hundred words or more.

Repeating the words or phrases over and over, literally hundreds of times, takes a great deal of patience, to be sure. However, there is an easy way to avoid this chore by recording the words on a phonograph record or a tape recorder. Then each day at lesson time, you bring the bird in its cage to the record player or tape recorder, and place it about a foot away from the speaker. Make sure that the volume is not too loud to disturb or frighten the bird. Though phonograph records are available for this purpose, it is more effective to use a record or tape of your own voice, with which the parakeet is familiar.

Teaching a budgie tricks is much easier than teaching him to talk. In fact, if you give him some toys to play with, he will invent his own tricks. He loves to climb up and down a miniature ladder, ride a little ferris wheel, and swing on anything that can be swung. If you hold out a cord horizontally—about a quarter-inch in diameter is the right size for his claws—he will walk or run across it, turn somersaults. If you hold it vertically from the top, he will climb up and down, performing these tricks with all the skill of a circus acrobat. During this brilliant act, it is unafraid because, if it should start to fall, it can instantly spread its wings and fly away without harm. Some people have their keet's wings clipped so that it cannot fly all over and perhaps get lost. But the owner who learns to love this lively, playful, and talkative creature would never have the heart to deprive it of its greatest natural gift—the power and graceful beauty of flight. You will get a lot more pleasure out of a parakeet if you let it be free as a bird.

Suggested Paperback Books:

Parakeets in Your Home, Mervin F. Roberts (New York: Sterling Publishing Co., Inc.), $1.25

Bringing up Budgie, Alice Sadler (New York: Sentinel Books Publ., Inc.), $1.00

Suggested Hard-cover Books:

Pet Book for Boys and Girls, Alfred Morgan (New York: Charles Scribner's Sons), $3.50

Forecasting the Weather

"Everybody talks about the weather, but nobody does anything about it," is a familiar saying often attributed to Mark Twain. However, it was actually written, back around 1890, by Charles D. Warner, a Connecticut newspaperman. In reality, today a great many people do something about the weather. In addition to the meteorologists at the United States Weather Bureau in Washington, and about 300 Weather Bureau offices throughout the country, there are over 12,000 reporting stations, largely manned by unpaid volunteers, who make daily weather, river, flood, and aviation weather observations. In the course of a year, well over a million general public weather forecasts are issued; nearly seven million preflight weather briefings are provided to airplane pilots;

and more than two hundred million telephone calls for weather information are answered by automatic telephones. Not too long ago, the weather was popularly believed to be unpredictable. However, with today's modern instruments, local forecasts for periods of from thirty-six to forty-eight hours are, in the main, highly accurate.

There are a number of factors which make weather observation an interesting, exciting, and enjoyable hobby. It gets you outdoors for a short period at least once a day, every day of the year, which is healthful, and also serves to develop the positive character traits of dependability and responsibility. There is the challenge of constantly testing the accuracy of your predictions against the actual results as they eventually become known. You always find out whether you were right or wrong. It is fun to keep a record of your hits and misses, checking one month against the next to discover how you are progressing. Should you later become an official volunteer observer, you will have the great satisfaction of knowing that you are contributing your bit to a highly essential national service which, in cases such as floods and flying weather, often saves lives. Meanwhile, by forecasting, you can plan outings for times when your observations predict favorable weather, thus being assured that, in most instances, you will have a good day for the hike, picnic, or whatever the occasion.

As is invariably advised throughout this book, always begin a new hobby in a modest way to save time and money until you have definitely decided that you wish to continue. The simplest and least costly way to start weather forecasting is to make observations with a weather vane and a barometer. The former costs only a couple of dollars, and less, of course, if you make it your-self. An aneroid barometer, which is the type with a cir-cular face like a clock, is the least expensive, costing around five dollars or so. All you need in addition is a table of wind and barometer indications for the United States, which will be found in the government publication, *Weather Forecasting,* listed below. To make a forecast with this simple equipment, you find the wind direction and read the barometer. Then, by referring to the table of indications, you will find the character of the weather for the next twelve to forty-eight hours.

After using this simple equipment until you are famil-ar enough with it to make predictions without referring to the table, you can add other equipment for measuring the speed of wind and the amount of precipitation in rain or snow. As you progress, you will also take into considera-tion the temperature, and learn to interpret the meaning of various cloud formations.

Weather observation is a rewarding hobby with many satisfactions. Though the familiar saying proclaims that "there's nothing new under the sun," and you might think that it surely applies to the weather, which is as old as the earth itself, actually there is always something new com-ing up in weather forecasting, and here is an amusing case in point.

A few years ago the Weather Bureau added what it called a Discomfort Index to its forecasts. This index tried to describe numerically the human discomfort re-sulting from the combined effects of temperature and moisture. Estimates showed that in the summer about ten per cent of the people would be uncomfortable even be-fore the index passed 70, and almost everybody would be uncomfortable, many feeling miserable, at 80 or above. Shortly after this Discomfort Index came into use, the Weather Bureau received many complaints. Merchants said that if a high index was reported, women wouldn't go shopping, preferring to try to keep cool at home. And beaches and other resorts complained that they, too, would lose patronage when uncomfortable weather was indicated. Under the circumstances, since the Weather Bureau does not falsify the facts, whatever the weather, there was only one thing that they could do: they changed the name of the index. So now it is called, as you know from listening to the weather reports on radio and television, the Temperature-Humidity Index, and merchants and resort owners no longer complain. However, it is still the same old Discomfort Index; but don't tell them or they may get up in arms again.

Suggested Paperback Books:

Weather Forecasting, Government Printing Office, Washington, D.C. 20402, 25 cents

Weather, Paul Lehr (New York: Golden Press, Inc.), 69 cents

Weather Forecasting as a Hobby, Robert Wells (Maplewood, N.J.: C. S. Hammond & Co.), $1.00

Suggested Hard-cover Books:

Our Changing Weather, Carroll L. and Mildred A. Fenton (Garden City, N.Y.: Doubleday & Co., Inc.), $2.95

Everybody's Weather, Joseph Gaer (Philadelphia: J. B. Lippincott Co.), $4.95

Insects

The study and collection of insects is an intriguing hobby which covers so wide and varied a field that there is always something different to look for. You can conduct field studies, you can raise them at home, or you can mount specimens in plastic boxes for display, butterflies and moths being particularly colorful.

Suggested Paperback Books:

Insects, Herbert S. Zim and Clarence A. Cottam (New York: Golden Press, Inc.), $1.00

Insect Fact and Folklore, Lucy W. Clausen (Riverside, N.J.: Collier Books), 95 cents

Insects Close Up, Edward S. Ross (Berkeley, Calif.: University of California Press), $1.50

Butterflies, Arthur Smith and Vernon Shearer (Baltimore: Penguin Books, Inc.), $1.65

Insects, Alice Gray (New York: Golden Press, Inc.), 50 cents

Suggested Hard-cover Books:

Butterflies, J. F. Gates (New York: Golden Press, Inc.), $2.95

Rocks and Minerals

If geology is your hobby, you will become increasingly interested in the natural world around you as you learn more about it. To you, a rock will not be just another rock, but an interesting specimen, perhaps millions of years old. The equipment you need is simple and costs relatively little: a geologist's hammer, a compass, a mag-

nifying glass, notebook and pencil, heavy gloves, and a
field bag.

Suggested Paperback Books:

Geology, Merit Badge Series (Boy Scouts of America), 35
    cents
Rocks and Minerals, Herbert S. Zim and Paul R. Shaffer (New
    York: Golden Press, Inc.), $1.00
Rocks, Eva Knox Evans (New York: Golden Press), 50 cents

Suggested Hard-cover Books:

Rocks and Their Stories, Carroll L. and Mildred A. Fenton
    (Garden City, N.Y.: Doubleday & Co., Inc.), $2.75
My Hobby Is Collecting Rocks, David E. Jensen (Chicago:
    Children's Press), $3.95
Story of Rocks & Minerals, David M. Seaman (Irvington-on-
    Hudson, N.Y.: Harvey House, Inc., Publishers), $3.50

The Bird Cure for Boredom

The most colorful natural life in the fields and the
woods is that of the birds. In recent years, more and more
people, of all ages, have taken up bird watching and find
it a sure cure for boredom. Here in the United States, the
best time for "birding" is about a month in spring, when
the migratory birds come north, and the same length of
time in the fall, when they head for southern climes.
You'll need a pair of binoculars, which cost from about
fifteen dollars up to several hundred dollars. Or perhaps
your Dad has a pair he'll let you borrow. If there isn't an
Audubon or other bird club in your locality, organize one

yourself. Never go into the woods alone as you may get lost. Always go with a group, and you will have an exciting time as you identify rare migratory birds, whether in city parks or country areas.

Suggested Paperback Books:

How to Know the Birds, Roger Tory Peterson (New York: Signet Books), 50 cents

Bird Watching as a Hobby, Robert Wells (Maplewood, N.J.: C. S. Hammond & Co.), 69 cents

Suggested Hard-cover Books:

Feathers and Flight, Clarence J. Hylander (New York: The Macmillan Company), $3.75

Giant Golden Book of Birds, Robert Allen (New York: Golden Press, Inc.), $3.99

Look for a Bird's Nest, Robert Scharff (New York: G. P. Putnam's Sons), $2.75

Sea Shells

Collecting sea shells is one of the most inexpensive of hobbies, for all you need is a small shovel and a bag. If you don't happen to have a shovel handy, just use your hands. The most important thing, of course, is an ocean; and though you don't live near one, very likely you visit a beach once or twice in the summer. The best time to "beachcomb" for mollusks is at low tide, and after storms when fresh specimens may be cast ashore. In just a few visits to the seaside, you should be able to find a good starting collection.

Suggested Paperback Books:

Sea Shells of the World, R. T. Abbott, Herbert S. Zim, ed.
(New York: Golden Press, Inc.), $1.00
Shellcraft Instruction, Marjorie & Frank Pelosi (Great Out-
doors Publishing Co.),$1.50

Suggested Hard-cover Books:

My Hobby Is Collecting Sea Shells, Ruth H. Dudley (Chicago:
Children's Press), $3.95
Story of Shells, Curtis Martin (Irvington-on-Hudson, N.Y.:
Harvey House, Inc.), $3.50

Terrariums

A terrarium can be made in a gallon fish bowl or in a
small fish tank. You will need sand for the bottom layer
of the tank, topped by a layer of charcoal. This should be
followed by a layer of top soil. Then put in some moss,
ferns, partridge berry, and wintergreen or other small
plants that you have found in the woods or bought in the
ten-cent store. Cover with a piece of glass, leaving space
for air to get in, and put in a salamander, or add a miniature lake for a turtle to swim in.

Suggested Paperback Books:

Gardening in Containers, edited by Sunset Magazine (Menlo
Park, Calif.: Lane Book Co.), $1.75

Suggested Hard-cover Books:

Fun Time Terrariums & Aquariums, Jerome Leavitt & John
Huntsberger (Chicago: Children's Press), $2.50

6

LET'S BE A CRAFTSMAN

No greater compliment can be paid a hobbyist in the arts and crafts than to say that he is "a fine craftsman." Manufacturers of quality items advertise with rightful pride that their products are made "with loving care." A good artisan is meticulous, being extremely precise about every little detail. He isn't satisfied until he has put the very best that is in him into the object he is fashioning. A good woodworker is said to have "a feel for wood." When he finishes something, it is not only well-made, but artistically designed as well. A craftsman working in plastic will keep on polishing a piece until there isn't a scratch on it, and it glows with a highly lustrous finish. A fine artisan isn't content with anything less than the best. To work in the arts and crafts, therefore, one must be careful and patient, and he must have high standards of quality and design.

If you have "a feel" for wood, leather, plastic, metal, or whatever the nature of the raw material, plus the characteristics mentioned, you will find craftsmanship both enjoyable and rewarding. When you make something useful and artistic, with your own hands, there is justifiable pride in a job well done. Another satisfaction from such a hobby is that you can make distinctive gifts for relatives and friends at appreciably less cost than if you bought the manufactured article. And, of course, you will make things for yourself. Many a man, who went into some phase of arts and crafts as a boy, has several things he made which he has treasured over the years.

Should you not have the facility for working with leather, plastic, and the like, you can still go in for one of the construction hobbies that require somewhat less expert handiwork. You can build a soapbox racer or construct model planes. You can make model cars from kits or run a model railroad. Or you can go in for the latest craze: slot-car racing, either building your own model or buying one, and racing it at the large tracks provided at hobby stores or on your own smaller track at home. The variety of things you can build or put together is practically limitless; so there is bound to be something in the area of the construction hobbies that will provide you with a great deal of entertainment, at least for the time being, or perhaps up into adulthood. Look through the selection in this chapter, also check the hobby books at the public library, and visit a hobby shop with its wealth of construction hobbies on display. Among this vast array, there is certain to be at least one interest that particularly appeals to you.

The World of Plastics

As a prime example of what can be done in arts and crafts, let us take plastic, since it is a relatively new material that can be processed in many ways. There are over fifty kinds of plastic in use today, and the articles made from it range all the way from a simple napkin holder for the dining table to important parts in rockets and space stations. In fact, it is expected that in the near future, both automobiles and homes will be largely built of plastic.

The most popular type of plastic for hobbyists is as clear as glass, and can be shaped either with tools or by heating. The trade names are "Lucite" and "Plexiglas," both having similar qualities. They can be worked with the same tools used for wood: saws, drills, sandpaper, and polishing machines. The plastic can be bought in sheets, blocks, and rods to suit every purpose. Prices run from a few cents to several dollars, depending, of course, upon the size.

In addition to being cut and drilled, plastic can be cast in molds, imbedding insects, coins, shells, and many other small objects. A collection of insects imbedded in plastic blocks makes a highly attractive display that can be handled without damage, and that will last for a lifetime and more. So, if you are a naturalist, you can thus make a most unusual and outstanding collection which will be admired by everyone.

Start, as with any other craft hobby, by making simple things: a desk blotter, napkin holder, or jewel box. Use plastic sheets ¼" thick and cut with a jigsaw to the proper dimensions. Then heat in accordance with directions given, and shape as desired. Affix parts together with plastic cement. Polish the article with sandpaper dipped in water. You can give it a high finish by polishing with cotton discs mounted on the shaft of a small motor. Easy-to-follow instructions are obtainable from hobby shops at little cost and often without charge. Use care and patience, and keep in mind that in the arts and crafts hobbies, the most important ingredient is loving care.

Suggested Paperback Books:

Casting in Clear Plastic, Elmer Holt (New York: American Handicrafts), 50 cents

Liquid Plastic Artistry (New York: American Handicrafts), 50 cents

How to Preserve Animals and Other Specimens in Clear Plastic (New York: American Handicrafts), $1.00

Suggested Hard-cover Books:

Plastic Magic, Carroll B. Colby (New York: Coward-McCann, Inc.), $2.50

Magic Mixtures: Alloys and Plastics, Philip Carona (Englewood Cliffs, N.J.: Prentice-Hall, Inc.), $2.95

Soap Sculpture

One of the most interesting and inexpensive ways to try your hand at sculpture can be practiced by using ordinary white soap as a medium. Use a large rectangular cake of soap to get as much working area as possible, and scrape down one side until you have a smooth area to work on. Then make drawings the size of the cake of the front and the sides of the subject you are sculpting. Select something simple, like an Indian, an animal, or a fish. Place the paper on the soap and, with an awl or a common pin, punch holes along the lines of the drawing to guide you. Then follow the outline by carving the soap along the pinholes with a small, pointed knife. Don't expect that your first efforts will get you an award. But keep at it and, as you improve with practice, work up to more intricate designs.

Suggested Paperback Books:

Sculpture, Remington Schuyler, Merit Badge Series (Boy Scouts of America), 35 cents

Tips on Soap Carving, National Soap Sculpture Committee, Box 202 Church Street Station, New York, N.Y., free

Working with Metals

They say that boys like to bang on things—and men do, too! Perhaps that is why metalwork is a popular hobby with males of all ages. Metals have their own particular characteristics and, if properly handicrafted, most of them can be made into attractive pieces; so the one you select depends upon your preference. Here are the metals popularly preferred by hobbyists:

ALUMINUM: A malleable metal that is readily hammered or etched. After being hammered, it must be annealed, heated, that is, over a gas plate, which is the simplest way, or with a bunsen burner or alcohol torch. After it has been shaped and designed, heat it until a piece of letter paper placed on it turns brown; then allow to cool of itself.

BRASS: Being harder than aluminum, copper, and pewter, brass is best for work requiring sawing and filing; select the softer metals for hammering.

COPPER: One of the most attractive and popular of

metals. Being quite soft, it can be hammered and shaped in many ways. The metal is placed over a wooden mold and hammered down into the shape of the design. You will need a ball peen hammer for this purpose. Then it is annealed to avoid cracking. First clean the copper with steel wool. Then, holding it carefully with a pair of pliers, pass it back and forth through the flame of a gas burner until it has turned an attractive color. Finally, wax while it is still warm, and when cool, polish with a soft cloth.

PEWTER: Perhaps the most popular of all handicraft metals, because it is malleable enough to work easily and has a soft, silvery finish which does not tarnish.

STERLING SILVER: Many beautiful pieces of jewelry and other objects may be made with this beautiful metal which has been admired for centuries. Though it is the most expensive of the popular metals, the cost is not prohibitive when the amount used is small.

Start working on metal with a minimum of tools; then if you really get enthusiastic about the hobby you can add to the basic requirements. All you need at first are a ruler, awl, saw, ball peen hammer, and a few files. Hobby supply houses provide the various metals in many shapes and sizes, so you don't have to bother to cut from rough stock. Designs and instructions for making a wide variety of simple pieces are provided free, and can also be found in catalogues and books on the subject.

For an easy-to-do initial project, make a candy dish, using pewter because it is so soft that it does not require annealing, and therefore needs only to be hammered. Purchase a circular piece of pewter 7" in diameter. With a compass, draw on it a circle 5" in diameter, and an inner circle 2″ in diameter, using the same axis point for your compass. You can use a wood mold with that size depression. However, the simplest and cheapest method is to make—it can be purchased if you prefer—a canvas bag about a foot square, partially fill it with sand, and sew up the open end. Make a depression in the bag and place the pewter disc over it. Hammer within the 2″ marked circle to form the base; then work out toward the 5″ circle. Keep turning the piece with your other hand as you hammer in order to shape the metal evenly all around. Should the edge of the dish get bent, flatten it with a wooden mallet; your mother may have a wooden potato masher which will do the job without harming the masher. You can make this candy dish in about an hour. Check to make sure that it stands evenly on a flat surface. Then wet some fine steel wool, rub it on soap, and polish the piece until it has an even shine. Now place the dish on a coffee table or buffet, and the only other thing you need is some candy to serve in it.

Suggested Paperback Books:

Metalwork, Merit Badge Series (Boy Scouts of America), 35 cents

A Treasury of Hobbies and Crafts, Michael Estrin, ed. (Baltimore: Ottenheimer Publishers, Inc.), $1.00

Suggested Hard-cover Books:

Fun with Metalwork, J. W. Bollinger (Milwaukee, Wis.: Bruce Publishing Co.), $4.75

Metal Craft, F. Johns (Hackensack, N.J.: Wehman Bros.), $1.75

Working with Wood

Primitive man naturally first worked with wood because it was available in abundance and, before metal was used for tools, the wood could be cut and shaped with sharp-edged stones. Woodworking has always been a popular hobby because it is easily managed, and today, with the wide variety of tools at hand, the number of things that can be made is almost limitless.

There are over thirty different species of wood usually found at lumber dealers. Of these, a half-dozen are commonly used by woodworkers:

BASSWOOD: Yellow or tan in color, with a close but soft grain. Frequently used for making toys.

CHESTNUT: Light brown in color, with a coarse grain, and relatively soft. Care must be taken that it does not split.

MAHOGANY: Usually red or brown, with a close, even grain, and not too hard. Not difficult to work with.

OAK: White, which is very hard; and red, which is less hard. This wood is strong, with a fairly close grain. Often used for carving.

WALNUT: Brown, very hard, with a smooth, close grain. Used in making fine furniture.

Obtain some small, waste pieces of these woods and work on them with knife, saw, files, and sandpaper to discover their qualities and how they act with various tools. All you will need at first is a good jackknife, a hammer, a crosscut saw, a coping saw, a half-round file, and sandpaper. Add other tools as your interest in this hobby develops. To get the feel of the tools and their use, start by making a few simple things.

Get a piece of wood a foot square and a quarter-inch thick. Stand on it in your stocking feet and draw their outline on the board. Cut out the two pieces with a compass or coping saw. Smooth off the edges with the flat side of the half-round file and finish with sandpaper. Cut four straps, ¼" wide, out of cloth, plastic, or leather. Nail them to the sides of the wood so that one strap goes over the base of the toes and the other over the instep. You now have a pair of beach or bathroom sandals which, though rough and ready, serve their purpose well. If you want to fancy them up a bit, stain or varnish the wood, and let dry before wearing.

For a pleasing outdoor decoration, take a piece of wood six inches square and ¼" thick, and draw a simple outline of a bird in flight. Cut this out with a saw, sandpaper, and then paint in brilliant, contrasting colors. Bore a hole in the center of the bird and insert a dowel stick about two feet long. Sharpen it at the lower end and stick in the lawn or a flower bed, where it will cause comment and be admired.

For something unusual in the way of personal adornment, make a few bolo ties to wear. A bolo, as you may know, is a Western-style tie worn around the neck, consisting of a cord which is held together by a decorative piece made of wood, plastic, or metal. The Montana and New Mexico pavilions at the New York World's Fair, 1964-65, displayed some very unusual bolos with beautiful ornaments made of wood and various metals, including silver.

To make a bolo—also called "gaucho"—tie to wear,

you will need a cord, a slide, and a pair of tips, all of which are available at handicraft supply stores. The cords come in various colors and are usually fifteen cents each; the slides are also fifteen cents apiece; and a pair of tips, usually 15 cents. So for an outlay of forty-five cents you can have a bolo tie which sells at retail for about $2.50. To begin making it, search around until you find a piece of prettily grained wood about two inches long and saw off a strip one-fourth inch wide. Work on this piece very carefully—so as not to break it—with sandpaper until it is as smooth as you can possibly make it and until it shows off the grain distinctly. Don't be disturbed if the wood breaks and you have to start all over, for this is a delicate operation. Then cover the wood with a light stain or a clear varnish. Now fasten the decoration to a slide with any all-purpose glue, insert the cord, and attach the tips. If you have taken pains and been patient, doing your very best, you will have an attractive bolo tie with an unusual handmade ornament that will gain you many compliments for your artistry.

As has been noted, the decorations can also be made of plastic or metal. One displayed at the World's Fair, that is easy to make, consisted of a copper piece in the shape of an arrowhead which, though simple, was very striking.

Suggested Paperback Books:

Wood—Colors and Kinds, Government Printing Office, Washington, D.C. 20402, 50 cents

Wood Handbook, Government Printing Office, Washington, D.C. 20402, $2.25

Woodcarving, E. J. Tangerman, Merit Badge Series (Boy Scouts of America), 35 cents

Wood Carving, edited by Sunset Magazine (Menlo Park, Calif.: Lane Book Co.), $1.95

Suggested Hard-cover Books:

Wood Carving, Freda Skinner (New York: Sterling Publishing Co., Inc.), $3.95

Modern Woodwork, Ralph J. Vernon (Austin, Tex.: Steck Co.), $1.20

The Printer's Devil

An apprentice in a printshop is commonly called a "printer's devil." Benjamin Franklin started his career as an apprentice in his brother James' printshop in Boston, when Ben was only twelve years old! And yet from that lowly position, he became, as you know, a distinguished statesman, scientist, and philosopher. He was also an inventor, a printer, and a writer. *Poor Richard's Almanack,* an American literary classic published for twenty-six years in the 1700's is still read, enjoyed, and appreciated well over two centuries later.

Printing is an ancient and honorable craft, receiving its greatest incentive more than five hundred years ago, when Johann Gutenberg invented the process of printing from movable type. Ever since then new methods of reproduction have been developed, speeding the process and making it simpler and cheaper. There is offset lithography which prints on paper from an inked impression on a rubber cylinder. There is the almost instantaneous

photographic reproduction done by the business machines
you have seen advertised on television.

What sort of fellow would be particularly interested in
printing as a hobby? He'd be a thoughtful chap, with an
eye for attractive design, believing in the spreading of information through words and pictures, and not averse to
getting his hands stained with ink. He might like to start
a modest weekly newspaper telling of the past and forth-
coming events of the neighborhood, combining the printing hobby with that of journalism.

Running a little newspaper can be a lot of fun. You can
do it all yourself, or, more ambitiously, it can be a group
project, with an editor, reporter, printer, and advertising
manager. You will meet many people, and they will get to
know you. More importantly, getting out a paper gives
you a sense of responsibility that will stand you in good
stead for the rest of your life.

The equipment needed runs into a little money, but not
too much. First, you'll want a typewriter, and an old one
can be picked up for as little as ten dollars, or perhaps it
can be borrowed. Amusingly enough, the fellow who has
a typewriter often is named the editor-in-chief, much as
the chap who owns the baseball is automatically made
the captain of the sandlot team. And though you don't
know how to type, don't let that disturb you. You can
learn as you go along, picking up speed and facility with
practice.

You will need some method of printing your paper, of
course, and regular printing presses, even small ones, are
expensive. But that needn't deter you, for today there
are several printing processes which cost as little as ten to
twenty-five dollars for equipment. You might pick up a

small hand-operated press secondhand, or use a mimeo-graph machine or some other kind of duplicator. Many a club paper has been started with an investment of as little as twenty-five dollars.

If you begin with a group, assign the various staff positions to those who are particularly qualified for the job. The reporter should have "a nose for news," and be on his toes in finding out what is going on of interest to the readers. The editor should be a fairly good grammarian and always keep a dictionary handy. The printer should be able to tinker with simple machinery, find out what's wrong, and fix it quickly. The advertising manager is important because he has to get people to pay cash for public notices or to advertise their wares. And the whole staff must be trying constantly to sell subscriptions, or single copies of the paper, to everybody.

Getting out a club or neighborhood newspaper is a whale of a lot of fun. It is exciting, you've got to be on the go, and you must get your paper out on time. Even if you don't go into some phase of the publishing business later on, the experience you gain is invaluable, whatever your vocation may be, and you will have many thrilling and pleasurable memories to reflect upon in the years to come.

There are numerous other areas of printing that you can investigate once you have a press or other machine for multiple reproduction. You can design your own greeting cards and print as many as you need. You can print announcements, posters, notices, and the like. You can do job printing for others. In the case of members of your family and close friends, you might do the work "for free." But in other instances, don't be hesitant in charging enough to cover your costs, plus a reasonable profit. Lots of boys who take up printing as a hobby earn extra money in this way. A good idea is to put these funds aside until you have enough to purchase a better printing press. Investigate the possibilities of being a "printer's devil." It will help to develop latent talents, you'll learn a lot that is new to you, and you will enjoy yourself immensely along the way.

Even without a machine there are inexpensive fonts of letters that can be purchased to use with an ink pad to make cards or announcements. There are helpful devices for aiding you in doing hand lettering for posters or flyers.

Suggested Paperback Books:

Printing, Merit Badge Series (Boy Scouts of America), 35 cents

Printing: Careers and Opportunities for You, Philip Pollack (Philadelphia: Chilton Co.), $2.50

Suggested Hard-cover Books:

First Book of Printing, Sam and Beryl Epstein (New York: Franklin Watts, Inc.), $2.50

Paper, Ink and Roller, Harvey Weiss (New York: William R. Scott, Inc.), $3.75

Cars, Trains, Ships, and Planes

Model construction has an immense following among "boys" of all ages, from eight to eighty. Principally because of the rapid advance in the uses of plastics, finished models and construction kits can be manufactured and sold at reasonable cost today. Some people arc simply collectors, buying finished models of ships, cars, or planes, and putting them on display. However, since no creativity or handicraft is involved, this hobby lacks excitement and the pleasure of construction. Therefore, most hobbyists in this area work either from raw materials and plans, or from kits.

If you haven't done model construction before, follow the basic rule which applies to all hobbies: start simply and gradually work up to the more intricate forms, making only a modest cash investment until you know for sure that a particular hobby will hold your interest for some time.

A common mistake is to begin with a kit that is difficult to construct; consequently a bad job is made of it. Such a disappointing experience often results in giving up the whole field of construction hobbies, once and for all, and thereby missing out on a lot of fun. If, say, your interest is in cars, it is better to buy several simple kits, each costing a dollar or even less, than to put all your money into one complicated kit that is beyond your present capability and experience to construct. Ambition is a fundamental characteristic, without which one cannot get ahead in any area of life, but try to restrain your natural enthusiasm, and don't be overambitious when starting on a construction hobby. Right now you have more leisure than you will have in later life, so take your time, and however modest the project, keep in mind that the important thing is to do a good job. A little car kit, costing only 79 cents, and carefully constructed, is much more to be admired than a large kit, costing ten times as much, which plainly shows that it has been botched in the building. A kit which offers some choice as to the appearance of the finished model is most creative.

As with all the other general hobby areas, the first step is the matter of selection since you want a hobby from which you, as an individual, will derive the most satisfaction in every way: enjoyment, knowledge, training, experience, and entertaining recreation. Don't rush into something that momentarily takes your fancy. Look over the vast field of construction hobbies and thoughtfully consider them all before making your own choice.

If you live beside the sea, and are fascinated by its many manifestations, if you like to go boating, and if you fish, then constructing model ships would be a logical choice.

Are you really interested in aviation? Have you ever flown in an airplane? Would you like to, or would you prefer to leave that form of transportation to the other fellow? In this space age, though aviation is of prime importance both commercially and defensively, still eight out of ten adults have never flown in a plane. But if you have flown or hope to fly, if you read about the constant progress in aviation, if you like fiction about flying, if you like to study the new designs as they are reported, then constructing model planes will be more than just another hobby to you because of your general interest in aviation.

Constructing and operating a model railroad has been a popular hobby for many years with both male juniors and adults. When you were quite young, you probably had a set of trains and tracks which you used as a boy. Now that you are older, you might wish to continue this hobby on a more elaborate basis. The investment can run anywhere from about twenty-five dollars for a modest power-operated set, up to the many hundreds of dollars, which some adult hobbyists spend, in accordance with their means.

Perhaps you have seen the largest model railroad in the world, in display at the New York World's Fair 1964-1965. It covers 3,000 square feet, with nearly three miles of track, 400 locomotives, 600 railway cars, 2,400 buildings, 8,000 figures of people, 12,000 lights. It took eight years to construct.

You will get the most pleasure out of this hobby if you use your ingenuity and imagination in developing a railroad system from your own ideas. Don't merely follow printed plans to construct one which is much the same as many others. Make your own layout to fit the room that you have available, lay the tracks, put up the buildings and other equipment, and then landscape it picturesquely. Building and operating a model railroad is a long-term project, so think it out carefully as you construct and expand it, to avoid a hodgepodge, and end up with something you can really be proud of. It takes time, effort, and money; but if you love the idea of railroading, it is well worthwhile.

Very nearly every boy is interested in cars, and expects to drive one, since automobiles are a prime adjunct in the family life of modern America. Model cars are, therefore, extremely popular as a hobby. There are hundreds of kits available, from simple ones, which can be put together in a matter of minutes, to highly complicated ones, which may take weeks of intense effort to construct. So take it easy, learn how to use the wide variety of tools skillfully, and don't be satisfied until you have built a model car that is outstanding in its workmanship, finished appearance, and smoothness of performance. Then you will be rewarded for the long, unstinting hours of labor by a thrill that you will never forget.

The collection of miniature models of cars is a branch of the model car hobby that is growing in popularity. Some of the miniatures are exact reproductions in detail of the larger cars.

Slot-Car Racing

The latest craze in model cars is racing them on electrified slotted tracks. Today there are 3½ million boys and men, manipulating hand-held controls, who operate their model cars at scale speeds of over 200 miles an hour. Since a stripped-down Ferrari or a Corvette Sting Ray costs less than three dollars, racing slot cars can be an inexpensive hobby. Small tracks can be bought for home use, but many enthusiasts like to race their cars on the large setups available at hobby shops and elsewhere; there is a slot-car track at the John F. Kennedy playground in Washington, D.C., and more are being constructed at other playgrounds. Start with an inexpensive stripped-down car and, as your enthusiasm grows, build your own and race it against those of your friends and acquaintances. You will really get a charge out of this latest development in the construction hobbies.

Suggested Paperback Books:

Model Kars, George Barris, AMT Corp., Box 400, Troy, Mich., 25 cents

Hobbies Are Family Fun, a catalogue, Polk's Hobby Dept. Store, 314 Fifth Ave., New York, N.Y., free

Model Railroading, Lionel Corp. (New York: Bantam Books), 95 cents

Suggested Hard-cover Books:

Model Boats for Beginners, Horace H. Gilmore (New York: Harper & Row, Publishers), $2.95

Airplane Model Building, Gene Johnson (Cambridge, Md.: Cornell Maritime Press), $3.00

How to Design and Build Flying Models, Keith Laumer (New York: Harper & Row, Publishers), $4.95

Model Railroading, Harry Zarchy (New York: Alfred A. Knopf, Inc.), $3.50

Boys' Book of Model Railways, Ernest Carter (New York: Roy Publishers), $3.00

Building and Operating Model Cars, Walter Musciano (New York: Funk & Wagnalls Co.), $3.50

7

LET'S LOOK AT SCIENCE

THE fastest growing hobbies today are in the field of science. People of all ages, and both sexes, are taking up some aspect of science as a hobby. The reason for its general popularity is that the area is so vast and varied that almost everyone can find a specialized science which interests him. For instance, if you are the outdoors type, you might like to investigate botany, geology, or zoology; if you are mathematically minded, you may become intensely interested in physics or the space sciences. Whatever your inclination, there is a good possibility that you can discover a branch of science which fascinates you.

Science hobbies are also popular because they afford an opportunity to be creative. If you have a large bump of curiosity, and want to know the "what, why, and how" of things, the chances are favorable that some phase of science can open up a whole new and wonderful world for you. And, too, unlike many other hobbies, a scientific bent may lead to a career which will constitute your life's work, and be most rewarding. What's more, there is lots of recreation and enjoyment to be found in a science hobby. In short, science has that basic quality which is found in all good hobbies—it is fun. And on top of these positive characteristics, also to be considered is the fact that our country and the world need scientists today as never before.

The foundation of all sciences is mathematics, so if you get good grades in that subject and, later on, in physics and other sciences, you have a definite advantage in exploring this hobby field. However, if mathematics puzzles you, as it does many students, this does not mean that you should not take up a science hobby. You don't have to plan to take up a scientific career to enjoy a science hobby now. You can get a lot of fun out of it by simply using it as a temporary pastime. And you may, meanwhile, discover to your surprise that you do have a talent for a certain branch of science after all. So survey the selection of science hobbies in this chapter, and consider them thoughtfully before you make up your mind.

The Oldest Science—Astronomy

Man has always looked up at the stars and planets and wondered about them. He saw them in the night sky, but hadn't the faintest idea of their purpose, their composition, or the vast distances that separate them. And in this scientific age, though man has learned much about the heavens, he continues to wonder, and there is still much that he doesn't know.

Ever since there have been ships, man has navigated by the stars. And he could not send explorers into space today were it not for the immense fund of knowledge gained by astronomers over thousands of years. So if you dream of becoming an astronaut, your best preparation is to take up astronomy as a hobby now.

The study of stars and planets is interesting, enjoyable, and relaxing; and the initial cost is little or nothing. To begin, select a clear night, place a blanket on the lawn, lie down on it, and look up at the vast array of heavenly bodies spread out above you. If you live in a city, go up on the roof, or to a park, if there is one nearby. The most comfortable way to study the heavens is in a beach chair with an adjustable back. If city lights interfere with your observations, get a mailing tube a foot or two long and use it as a rudimentary telescope. You can make a satisfactory one by simply rolling up a sheet of heavy paper and holding it in shape with rubber bands or glue.

To help you locate and recognize the constellations, planets, and stars, obtain some seasonal star charts and planet tables, which cost very little. You will also find them in books on astronomy; see *Stars,* by Zim and Baker, listed below. As you find the constellations, check them off on the star charts. Continue these observations until you have located a dozen or so of the brightest stars and about twenty-five constellations, and can readily find them, when you will have the pleasure of quickly identifying them and pointing them out to others.

After this preliminary phase as an amateur astronomer, if your interest continues, you will want to have some optical means of increasing your knowledge and enjoyment of the heavens. There are two types of telescopes. The simpler is the refractor telescope, consisting of a large lens, called the objective, at one end of a tube, which focuses the light at the other end, where the image is magnified by a smaller lens, called the eyepiece or ocular. In the other type, called the reflector, the light is gathered by a mirror, and the image is magnified by the eyepiece.

Telescopes may use either principle. Binoculars consist of two telescopes, which can usually be focused simultaneously, mounted on a single frame.

The cost of these optical instruments runs from about five dollars up to several hundred. Telescopes are usually less expensive than binoculars of the same magnification and quality. Today a good ten-power, American-made telescope can be purchased for about ten dollars. Binoculars range from twenty dollars and upwards. The most useful size for general purposes is 7x35. The first number is the power, which is the ratio of magnification, which means that in this case, an object seventy feet away is magnified so that it is viewed as if it were only ten feet away. The second number is the diameter in millimeters of the objective lens. In selecting a pair of binoculars, be careful to avoid imitations that are not true prism binoculars; if the center of the eyepiece is on a direct line with the center of the objective, the instrument is an imitation and of little or no practical value.

With binoculars or a telescope, you can, naturally, see celestial bodies you have previously observed with the naked eye, larger and more clearly. And you will, of course, discover many more stars, thus heightening the thrill of your exploration of the heavens.

To extend your experience as an amateur astronomer, visit one of the planetariums which are now to be found around the country. Also consider joining a club of amateur astronomers, where you can exchange views and gather information. You may also like to try making a telescope yourself. The most popular among amateurs is the reflecting type. Kits with complete instructions are available at hobby stores, camera, and optical shops.

Suggested Paperback Books:

Stars, Herbert S. Zim and Robert H. Baker (New York: Golden Books), $1.00

Astronomy Made Simple, Meir H. Degani, Made Simple Books (Garden City, N.Y.: Doubleday & Co., Inc.), $1.45

Radio Astronomy & How to Build Your Own Telescope, John Heywood (New York: Arco Publishing Co., Inc.), 95 cents

Science Materials Center Catalog, Science Materials Center, Inc., 59 Fourth Ave., New York, N.Y., free

Book Counter Catalog, Adler Planetarium & Astronomical Museum, 1200 So. Lake Shore Drive, Chicago 5, Ill., free

How to Use Your Telescope, Edmund Scientific Co., 101 E. Gloucester Pike, Barrington, N.J., 60 cents

Earth and Beyond, Cornell Science Leaflet, Mailing Room, Stone Hall, Cornell University, Ithaca, N.Y., 20 cents

Suggested Hard-cover Books:

Boys' Book of Astronomy, Patrick Moore (New York: Roy Publishers), $3.00

When the Stars Come Out, Robert H. Baker (New York: Viking Press), $4.50

Experiments in Sky Watching, Franklyn M. Branley (New York: Thomas Y. Crowell Co.), $3.50

First Book of Astronomy, Vivian Grey (New York: Franklin Watts, Inc.), $2.50

If Invention Appeals to You

One important reason for searching through the almost limitless world of hobbies, which you are doing by reading this book, is to discover what particular facilities or talents you may have which can be developed so that you will enjoy a fuller, richer life. Many people never find a hidden talent they possess, or learn of it too late to do much, if anything, about it. This results in a lag that holds back progress more than it need be. The more a nation makes use of the potentialities of its citizens, the greater, more progressive, more prosperous it will be. That is why you should find out whether or not you have the type of mind which lends itself to the inventive process. Here is a test which will help you to decide:

1. Do you have a large "bump of curiosity"?

2. Do you like to take things apart to find out what makes them tick?

3. Do you try to find better ways of doing things?

4. Do you like to "just putter around" with objects, tools, and gadgets?

5. Do you believe that you have a good imagination?

6. Are you handy with tools?

7. Are you mechanically minded?

8. Instead of merely taking radio and television for granted, are you constantly awed and amazed at the wonder of transmitting the human voice and pictures through the atmosphere?

9. Are you the type of person who does not take things for granted?

10. Though you presently know little or nothing about invention, does it have any appeal to you as a hobby?

If you answer four or more of these questions in the affirmative, you have the kind of mental makeup favorable to the inventive process; and, of course, the higher your score, the more progress you will make in this fascinating hobby.

To many inventors, even those who have patented some of their ideas, invention is a part-time hobby or avocation. There are few who devote their whole time to it, most having some other vocation, which is the major source of their income. Because of these factors, plus the fact that it is highly creative, invention is a true hobby of the best caliber, and thus most rewarding in enjoyment, increasing knowledge, new experiences, and the thrill of developing what may turn out to be an original and useful idea. In addition to these rewards, you have certainly heard and read of inventors, past and present, who made a fortune. However, in this book, we purposely avoid discussing the money that might be made from some hobbies since we are here only concerned with their value in pleasure, knowledge, and fun. Later on, when you are choosing your career in life, you can consider whether or not one of your hobbies provides the opportunity of gaining some financial return. Meanwhile, insofar as invention is concerned, you might make note of the fact that in addition to the inventors who have become millionaires, there are many more who have never made a penny from their patented inventions.

One of the most interesting things about this field of endeavor is that in contrast to other areas, inventors come from all walks of life—from laborers to lawyers, from bakers to bankers, from handymen to housewives. Though education is of value in all fields, many inventors have had little or no formal education whatever, an outstanding example being Thomas Edison, whose schooling was limited to three months, after which he became a newsboy on a railroad. On the other hand, there are, of course, many successful inventors who have been highly educated.

How to Invent

An invention is, briefly, a new and useful device or contrivance which has been conceived or made by the original effort of its creator. The two most important words, which should always be kept in mind, are "new" and "useful." A thing must fulfill both these qualifications in order to be an invention. A new toy, for example, is considered useful since it provides recreation and pleasure. In this connection, note that a new and useful improvement on an older idea may also be considered as an invention, and, in fact, in the large-scale development of modern science, many new and useful improvements are invented today which are based on previous inventions. For example, such common and simple devices as can openers, clothes hangers, and ball-point pens, to mention but a few, continue to be improved upon by inventors.

Now how do you invent? At first you don't need any tools or equipment whatever, not even pencil and paper. All you require is curiosity and imagination. Start by picking up anything at all and examining it closely. Let us begin with a knife and fork and find out how observant you are. Put a plate on the table, with the fork on the left, the knife on the right. Now without touching them, mentally review how you use these items. Which do you pick up first: the knife or the fork? Do you take the knife in your left hand or the right? Which hand do you cut the food with? Go through the whole eating process in your imagination. Only then, pick up the utensils and go through the motions and check to see if you were right.

In America, those who are right-handed hold the fork in the left hand, and cut the meat with the knife held in the right hand. Then they put the knife down, and transfer the fork from the left hand to the right, and pick up the food. When they want to cut some more meat, they transfer the fork back to the left hand, pick up the knife, and cut some more food. After that, they put the knife down again, transfer the fork to the right hand, and continue eating. Doesn't that seem a rather complicated and clumsy method to use in transferring food from the plate to the mouth?

In Europe, people keep the fork in the left hand, and the knife in the right; and they do not transfer these utensils from one hand to the other in the process of eating. That is a simple solution; but it is difficult, if not impossible, to change the eating habits of a nation. So what can be done about improving the way we Americans eat? The moment you ask yourself that question, you have begun the inventive process.

To an inventive mind, the obvious answer is to make one utensil do the work of two. By designing a combination knife-and-fork, you can cut and pick up food with either hand, thus making it unnecessary to keep transferring a fork and knife from one hand to the other. This can be done in either of two ways. You can sharpen the outside edge of the first and fourth tines of the fork so that it can be used as a knife as well; or you can cut some tines at the end of the knife so that it can also be used as a fork.

Exactly the same creative process is used, no matter what you are trying to invent or improve upon. Take a simple toy like a hoop, for instance. You can take two hoops, placing one inside the other at right angles, and fastening them together so that they will stay in the same position. You now have a double hoop with the added qualities of a ball, which can be rolled in several directions, and won't fall down.

There is absolutely no limit to the possibilities in the field of invention. Take an ordinary suit hanger from a clothes closet. You place your jacket over the hanger and fold your trousers over the crossbar. Upon occasion, you will likely find that your trousers have slid off the bar and fallen on the closet floor. Surely there must be some better way of making a clothes hanger. New ideas in hangers are being designed, year in and year out, and in thousands of other items, too. Just wander through a variety, hardware, or department store and you will see them on every hand.

Being inventive in your thinking is the best way to develop your creative talents. Later on, when you are engaged in your chosen vocation, you will find that it is the creative person who gets ahead. Inventiveness is of value in every field of endeavor. Executives in business and industry must constantly work out new and better ways of doing things. Chemists in pharmaceutical laboratories regularly formulate new drugs. Whatever the nature of your career, you will have an exciting, enjoyable life if you are inventive, and you may well leave a heritage that is beneficial to mankind.

Later on, if your interest in invention as a hobby continues, you will want to investigate the possibility of patenting some of your ideas. Any inventor, regardless of sex or age, may apply for a patent. Remember that your invention must be new as well as useful. Many ideas, upon investigation, are found to have been previously invented and patented by someone else. The U. S. Patent Office receives roughly 100,000 applications a year, of which nearly half are denied, frequently because they have been thought of and patented before.

When you have worked out an idea which seems new and useful, make a sketch of it and describe it in simple terms. Then discuss it with your parents. If it is agreed that your invention seems to have merit, a search must be made to determine if it has been previously patented; this service costs from about five to twenty-five dollars. If the search indicates that your idea appears to be new and original, then application for a patent may be made. The cost is thirty dollars for filing, plus a final fee of thirty dollars if the application is allowed. If the services of a registered patent attorney are used, he naturally must be paid for his services. After a patent has been issued, it is of no value unless it can be sold to a company that will manufacture and merchandise it. This is a long and complicated process with which you need not be presently concerned. Meanwhile, enjoy invention as a hobby which, even if you never get a patent, can be of great value to you now, and in all the years ahead.

Suggested Paperback Books:

Patents and Inventions, Government Printing Office, Washington, D.C. 20402, 15 cents

The American Patent System, Government Printing Office, Washington, D.C. 20402, 20 cents

The Patent System All Around You, Patent, Trademark and Copyright Foundation, George Washington University, Washington 6, D.C., 12 cents

Invention, P. F. Collier & Son Corp., 640 Fifth Ave., New
    York, N.Y., 25 cents

Suggested Hard-cover Books:

The Sources of Invention, John Jewkes and others (New York:
    St. Martin's Press), $4.25
Young Inventors' Guide, Raymond F. Yates (New York:
    Harper & Row, Publishers), $2.95
3100 Needed Inventions, Raymond F. Yates (New York:
    Funk & Wagnalls Co.), $3.50

Magic and Mathematics

You may be surprised to learn that magic is a science
based on mathematical principles. The magician appar-
ently defies natural laws. We know that an object cannot
be made to disappear, and yet a magician can do it with
ease. Though we are certain that one solid cannot be
passed through another, a magician passes a coin through
a handkerchief with no difficulty whatever. We are positive that no one can read our thoughts, but a magician
is readily able to do so—or so it would appear.

A magician makes the impossible seem possible. He is
able to do so only because he uses mathematics and physical principles. Tricks with rope, string, and paper use the
laws of physics; tricks with coins and playing cards use
the law of probabilities for their successful performance.
Coins are numerical counters, and so are playing cards,
most card games having a mathematical structure. Once
you appreciate the fact that magic is based on science,
and is not just a lot of hocus-pocus, you can become an

accomplished amateur magician. Besides being fun for
the performer, and entertaining for the audience, magic
is of value in making you at ease with other people, and,
helps you to develop confidence in yourself—two positive
characteristics that are advantageous in promoting the
success of a career in any endeavor.

Suggested Paperback Books:

Magic Made Easy (Baltimore: Ottenheimer Publishers, Inc.),
    49 cents
Magic Tricks, Guy Frederick (New York: Sterling Publishing
    Co., Inc.), $1.00
Magic Tricks and Card Tricks, Wilfred Johnson (New York:
    Dover Publications, Inc.), $1.00
Quick and Easy Guide to Magic, Hal G. Vermes (Riverside,
    N.J.: Collier Books), $1.45

Suggested Hard-cover Books:

Magic, Harry Clarke (New York: Roy Publishers), $3.50
More Fun with Magic, Joseph Leeming (Philadelphia: J. B.
    Lippincott Co.), $3.25
First Book of Magic, Edward Stoddard (New York: Franklin
    Watts, Inc.), $2.50

Other Paperback Science Books:

Good books on the sciences run into the hundreds, and
every public library has a wide selection. It is also suggested that you visit a paperback bookstore and browse
in the science section. There are far too many titles to list,
but here are just a few which have been published under

the sponsorship of Science Service, a nonprofit corporation, for the popularization of science:

Wonderful World of Science, Shirley Moore and Judith Viorst (New York: Bantam Books), 50 cents

The Chemical Elements, Helen Miles Davis (New York: Ballantine Books, Inc.), 50 cents

150 Science Experiments Step-by-Step, Judith Viorst (New York: Bantam Books), 60 cents

Science Projects Handbook, Shirley Moore, ed. (New York: Ballantine Books), 50 cents

Science Sets

There are so many science sets and kits available that they need only be mentioned here. About everything you can think of is to be found today: chemistry, electronics, physics, microscope and telescope sets, nature kits, and many more. Prices range from a dollar to twenty-five dollars and up. If you haven't done so recently, visit a hobby store soon, feast your eyes on the wealth of scientific sets, and ask for copies of their catalogues.

Science Clubs

If you are science-minded, you can get a great deal of help in your hobby by joining or starting a science club. The Science Clubs of America, which has over a million members, is dedicated to the development of science interest and talent through its affiliated clubs in the United States and other countries, and seeks to stimulate an increasing knowledge and understanding of science. You can enter your class, group, or club for affiliation with the

Science Clubs of America without charge. Your sponsor can be either a science teacher, parent, adult leader, or a professional scientist. To obtain an application, write to Science Clubs of America Affiliation, 1719 N Street, N.W., Washington, D.C. 20036.

8

LET'S BE A GOOD SPORT

Whatever hobbies anyone may have, whether young-ster or adult, one of them should be a sports activity. A sport is an all-inclusive hobby because, in addition to be-ing spirited and enjoyable, it is healthful, as well; and if it is played in the open, as many are, there are the addi-tional benefits of exercising pleasurably outdoors, an op-portunity which city people, in particular, are not often afforded.

Other hobbies may be discarded in a few years, as you grow up and your interests change, but a sports activity is often continued into adulthood. The longer you play an athletic game, the more proficient you get. Therefore, in-stead of your interest waning, it intensifies as you get bet-ter and better. Once you have become a proficient swim-mer, you can take up skin and scuba diving; as a bowler you strive to increase your average score, hoping to roll 200, at least upon occasion; in golf, you first attempt to break 100, then try to score par, and eventually break par. The point is that in sports the challenge is always there, whether you play in your teens or in middle age. Thus the fascination is kept at a high level as you try to improve your score or play in competition against others.

An active sport is an important part of a general physical fitness program, which everyone should faithfully follow throughout life. Regular morning calisthenics is another fundamental factor. Such formal daily exercise isn't much fun, frankly, whereas a sports activity, enthusiastically performed, is refreshing, exciting, thrilling, and enjoyable. But keep in mind that you will get more out of it, and do better, by continuing your morning calisthenics, which serve to condition your whole body for the various physical activities, from work to play, that you engage in from day to day.

What Sport Is Best for You?

We can't all hope to be muscular strong men at the circus, nor would most of us care to be. It goes without saying, some persons have stronger constitutions than others. However, all those in reasonably good health should have a sports hobby unless the family physician advises against it. In fact, those who are less robust have all the more reason for practicing a sports activity to build themselves up, though they should select one which requires only a relatively modest expenditure of energy. Here then is a selection of popular sports, separated into their energy-expending values:

MODERATE ENERGY EXPENDITURE

Archery	Hiking (at a moderate pace)
Badminton	Horseback riding (at a walk)
Bicycling (moderate)	Horseshoes
Canoeing (moderate)	Ice skating (slow)
Golf	Roller skating (slow)

Shuffleboard   Swimming (breast and
Softball   back stroke)
                                              Table tennis

HIGH ENERGY EXPENDITURE

Basketball   Roller skating (fast)
Bicycling (fast)   Rowing
Bowling   Skiing
Handball   Swimming (crawl)
Horseback riding (at a trot)   Tennis
Ice skating (fast)   Volleyball

When people are young, they are inclined to be over-enthusiastic, especially boys. That is all to the good, for it heightens interest and excitement; but it should not be permitted to get out of control, especially in the field of active sports. So, if you are not a Samson, select a sport that expends a modest amount of energy. Such an activity has several advantages in that it can be played without undue strain and with little or no risk of injury to your still growing body. It can also be enjoyed without interruption for a longer period. For example, though an hour of bowling or a few sets of tennis are enough of a workout, after which one should quit for the time being, one can bicycle moderately or hike leisurely all day long without knocking oneself out. Therefore, select a sport that requires moderate energy, or high energy, in accordance with the state of your constitution. The activities in either classification are so varied that you have a wide choice.

Pick a sport that fits in with your way of life and balances your other interests, thus helping you to develop into a well-rounded person. For instance, if you don't do much walking, like most people in this motorized age, you might take up golf, because it will develop your leg muscles while you're having fun at the same time. Or if you are among that vanishing class of students who walk quite a way to school each day, as your grandparents did, then you might select archery or horseshoes, which calls for less legwork. If you are indoors much of the time, then select an outdoor sport; and vice versa. Choose a sport that fits in with your personal characteristics. If you are not easily ruffled, go horseback riding or play golf; whereas if you are inclined to get frustrated, try a relaxing sport like shuffleboard, horseshoe pitching, or canoeing. And if you are alone a great deal, select a team sport like softball in order to associate with others. Note that although the American Medical Association approves of softball for preteen-agers, it does not recommend the playing of regular baseball until the later teens, when the body has almost reached its full growth. Last but not least, after the foregoing considerations, choose a sport that you feel will be a lot of fun.

Archery

Man first used the bow and arrow to hunt game in order to feed his family; later it also served as a military weapon. Archery, the oldest of all existing sports, developed from this source; and the National Archery Association, founded in 1879, is the first amateur sporting organization established in the United States.

Archery is an excellent family sport since both sexes and all ages can play. A range can be set up almost anywhere, in a backyard or even in a family room, since the shooting distances run from only fifteen feet for beginners to twenty-five feet for more experienced archers. It is of particular interest to handicrafters since you can make your own bow, and kits can be purchased for this purpose.

Archery requires concentration, a good eye, a steady hand, and the strength to pull back the bowstring without losing your aim. In buying a bow, select one with a pull which is not too weak or too strong for you; as you get older and become more expert, you will need a bow with a heavier pull. In competition, play with boys of about your own age so that everyone has a fair chance. You can also compete with girls since, on short ranges, they can often score as well as boys. The cost of a complete junior archery set, including the target, is around ten dollars; it is naturally less if, as suggested, you make your own bow.

Suggested Paperback Books:

Beginning Archery, Roy K. Niemeyer (Belmont, Calif.: Wadsworth Publishing Co., Inc.), 75 cents

Archery, Edmund H. Burke (New York: Arco Publishing Co., Inc.), 95 cents

Bows and Arrows, Saxton T. Pope (Berkeley, Calif.: University of California Press), $1.50

Basketball

Curiously enough, baseball, derived from the English games of rounders and cricket, is often called "the Great American Game," whereas actually the truly "Great American Game" is basketball, which is one of the only two popular sports—the other is volleyball—that were originated in this country. Both were invented by the YMCA, and are now in the official Olympic Games program.

There are several reasons for the immense popularity of basketball. The rules are simple, and a person watching it for the first time can readily understand the play; the area is relatively small so that it is easy to follow the action from any seat; and most important of all, it is the fastest game played on foot. Though hockey and polo are faster, they are played on skates and on horseback, respectively. And on top of all that, basketball is as exciting for the spectators as it is for the players. In fact, after a game the spectators often collapse from exhaustion whereas the players still seem full of pep and rarin' to go.

Whatever your present growth, you can play basketball, though ten-to-twelve-year-olds require professional supervision. The principal safety rule is to play against fellows of about your own size. This holds true, of course, in all team competition. Since basketball requires high agility and endurance, better have a checkup by your family doctor, and consult your parents and your physical education instructor, before taking it up. And even if it is not for you, or if you don't care to be an active participant, you can still get a whale of a lot of pleasure out of being an enthusiastic basketball fan.

Suggested Paperback Books:

Basketball for Boys, Chuck Orsborn (Chicago: Follett Publishing Co.), $1.00

Basketball for Everyone, Clare Bee (New York: Ace Books, Inc.), 35 cents

Basketball: The Modern Way, J. G. Garstang (New York: Cornerstone Library, Inc.), $1.00

Suggested Hard-cover Books:

Sports and Games, Harold Keith (Riverside, N.J.: Crowell-Collier Press), $4.50

Bowling

The most popular and fastest growing sport today is bowling, there being well over thirty million who roll a ball down a lane in the hope of knocking down all ten pins and getting a strike. Of all bowlers, one-third—ten million, that is—range from ten to nineteen years of age.

What is there about bowling which fascinates both men and women, young and old? First, since the lanes are indoors, and today most of them are air-conditioned, it can be played in comfort throughout the year. The basic rules are simple, an important factor in determining the popularity of a game because anyone can understand them and have fun the very first time they play. Bowling is healthful, providing good exercise for both the arms and legs. The amount of agility and endurance required is moderate, so participants of all ages can play several games without knocking themselves out. Families can play together, the younger members being given handicaps. The costs of equipment and for playing fees are moderate. Competition between individuals or teams can reach a high pitch and become very exciting.

Bowling lanes provide instruction without charge. Bowling balls and score sheets are included in the fee, which is usually fifty cents per game. Bowling shoes are rented for twenty-five cents. Later, if you become enthusiastic about the game, you can purchase your own ball, about fifteen dollars, and your own shoes, under ten dollars.

When you first visit a bowling establishment, ask for a light-weight ball, which runs about ten pounds. Later, as your growing strength increases and your game improves, you can use a heavier ball. Pick up the ball, holding it in both hands, and stand at the foul line with your back to the pins. Take four and one-half steps and turn around. You are now in the proper position for rolling a straight ball. With a long, easy swing, as you walk toward the foul line, roll, don't throw, the ball down the center of the lane toward the pins. Very likely the ball will turn off and roll down the gutter, missing all the pins. But don't be discouraged. As in all games requiring some degree of skill, the first results are bound to be disappointing. It is crucial at this point, that the rank amateur doesn't say, "Aw, shucks!" and give up in disgust. Jimmy Demaret, member of golf's Hall of Fame, points out that if a boy tries to drive a golf ball before he knows how, he may do so badly that he never really tries to learn the game, missing out on a lot of fun thereby. This is also true of bowling and all other sports. The player who succeeds is the one who keeps up his gumption, and doesn't give up, no matter how poorly he plays in the first few sessions. This determination, this do-or-die spirit, is a critical factor in attaining success, whether it be in sports recreation, other hobbies, or one's lifetime vocation. Hold to that positive attitude, and you will reap its rewards in the attainment of your aims.

Suggested Paperback Books:

Quick and Easy Guide to Bowling, Hal & Jean Vermes (Riverside, N.J.: Collier Books), $1.50
AMF Guide to Natural Bowling, Victor Kalman (New York: Permabooks), 35 cents
Bowling for Boys and Girls, John J. Archibald (Chicago: Follett Publishing Co.), $1.00

Suggested Hard-cover Books:

Bowling, Charles Hall & others (New York: Sterling Publishing Co., Inc.), $1.95

Golf

The "ancient and honorable game" of golf has many factors in its favor. It is played outdoors on beautifully landscaped grounds; in an 18-hole game, the player walks nearly four miles; there is a constant challenge in hitting a little ball toward a small cup 1,000 feet (more or less) away; the basic rules are simple; although players sometimes blow up after making a poor shot, golf etiquette calls for good manners on the course; it is a companionable game resulting in many friendships; since it requires but a moderate expenditure of energy, it is not an exhausting game; it is healthful; and finally, if you don't take it too seriously, it's fun.

A decided advantage, well worth considering, is that golf affords an opportunity to earn extra money during the summer vacation, and you can learn the fundamentals of the game at the same time by observing the players you caddy for. Many professional players started out as caddies. Besides, in the commercial world, being a fair golfer is almost a "must" since business is often discussed in the clubhouse after a game.

A complete set of clubs consists of four woods, ten irons, and a putter, which, with a bag and some balls, can well cost a hundred dollars and more. However, many players learn the rudiments of the game with just four clubs: one wood, a couple of irons, and a putter, that run fifteen dollars or so, but you can sometimes pick up a second-hand set for around five dollars.

It is important not to buy an expensive set because the proper length of the shaft of the clubs depends upon your height; and in a year or two, as you continue growing and get taller, your first set of clubs will be too short for you. So don't invest any more than necessary in equipment until you have reached your full height; then, if your interest in the game continues—and chances are good that it will, since golf is enjoyed by millions—you can consider purchasing a larger and better set for fifty dollars, less or more, depending upon the state of your finances.

A standard course consists of eighteen holes, but you can play only the front or back nine; or you can play a nine-hole course, of which there are many, where, because it is shorter, the green fee is naturally less. Fees on public courses are usually fifty cents, seventy-five cents, up to a dollar or two per game. There is just one caution to keep in mind: below the age of fourteen, play only nine holes at a time; after that, go the full eighteen holes, if you wish. As for learning the game, if your dad is a golfer, ask him if he would give you a few basic lessons. You can practice putting outdoors on the lawn or indoors on a rug. However, never practice your swing—except on a driving range or a course—with a regulation golf ball, for you might accidentally damage property or seriously injure someone; instead, use the soft practice balls that are perfectly safe in limited areas.

In addition to practice, observe good players, as either a caddy or an invited spectator. Jimmy Demaret, previously mentioned, says that he learned by watching and then trying to duplicate the player's form. To quote a familiar bit of advice given nearly two thousand years ago: "Go and do thou likewise," and you should turn out to be a good golfer, enjoying this fine old sport throughout your whole life.

Suggested Paperback Books:

Beginning Golf, Ben Bruce and Evelyn Davies (Belmont, Calif.: Wadsworth Publishing Co., Inc.), 75 cents
Beginner's Guide to Golf, Bob Toski (New York: Grosset & Dunlap, Inc.), $1.00
Golf at a Glance, Willard Gaskill (New York: Arco Publishing Co., Inc.), $1.00
Getting Started in Golf, Doug Ford (New York: Cornerstone Library, Inc.), $1.00

Suggested Hard-cover Books:

Young Sportsman's Guide to Golf, Don Smith (New York: Thomas Nelson & Sons), $2.75

Tennis

Tennis was originally played by the kings of France and their attendants. Later, when kings were executed, the game naturally lost its popularity. It wasn't revived until nearly a hundred years ago, when a British army officer devised a game called "spharistike," which was played on a lawn with a net, rackets, and a ball. It doesn't seem possible that a game with that jaw-cracking Greek name would ever have become popular. Fortunately, though, the originator changed it to "tennis-on-the-lawn," and today it is played by millions of men and women, young and old.

Tennis is a vigorous game, requiring plenty of agility, endurance, and lots of leg work. However, a boy who has kept himself in good physical condition can start playing at the age of ten. And if you really go for the game, you may still play it when you are seventy or older.

Tennis is one of the most inexpensive of games since most amateurs play on public courts, available in every community, which charge but a small fee. The only equipment needed is a few balls and a racket, the latter costing from three dollars or so up to around ten dollars. When you are seriously interested in tennis, it is advisable to purchase a good racket; if you take care of it, and have it repaired when necessary, it will last for years.

If you are the type who likes to play hard and invites strong competition, then tennis is the game for you. Should you prefer a sport requiring only moderate energy expenditure, try archery or golf. In selecting a sport, choose one which fits your temperament and constitution. Whatever your sports hobby, learn to play well, but don't knock yourself out. Remember that the prime purpose of taking up sports or any other hobby is enjoyment and fun. Any other benefits there may be, such as exercise, health, getting outdoors, are plus values.

Suggested Paperback Books:

How to Play Better Tennis, William Tilden (New York: Cornerstone Library, Inc.), $1.00

Instant Tennis, Dick Bradlee (New York: Cornerstone Library, Inc.), $1.00

Lawn Tennis, Mike Davies (New York: Arco Publishing Co., Inc.), 95 cents

Suggested Hard-cover Books:

Young Sportsman's Guide to Tennis, Helen Jacobs (New York: Thomas Nelson & Sons), $2.75

Water Sports

Swimming is one of the best all-around sports because it exercises all parts of the body to an approximately equal degree. If you swim, you won't have sturdy legs and thin arms, or vice versa, for the arms and legs are developed in proportion. Therefore, when you see a good swimmer poised on a diving board, whether he is short or tall, slender or stocky, he is sure to have a well-balanced physique—a condition which everyone should strive for.

It goes without saying that swimming is healthful and good fun. However, what some people don't realize is that the ability to swim reasonably well is an important safety measure which may save one's life. A boy as young as five years of age may accidentally fall into a pond or other body of water. If he can at least dog paddle, he can keep his head above water until he is rescued; otherwise he may drown.

Those who cannot swim should never go on or into the water. This fundamental rule should always be observed. Yet many overlook it, and lose their lives thereby. If you want to enjoy water sports, first learn to swim. It is wise to take a few lessons from a qualified instructor, either at a beach or an indoor pool, such as those found at YMCA's and elsewhere.

When you have overcome any natural fear of the water, and can float and swim, you are ready to take up diving, boating, canoeing, and water skiing. At the age of twelve or more, you can try skin and scuba diving. In the former, a face mask, snorkel, and swim fins, commonly called "flippers," are used; a junior set costs about three dollars. The equipment for scuba diving calls for a face mask, a connecting hose to a tank of compressed air strapped to the back, and flippers for maneuverability; a scuba outfit costs nearly a hundred dollars, but most people rent them. Skin and scuba diving should not be attempted without supervised training; the YMCA conducts training programs in these twin sports, and a medical examination is required of all candidates.

Whatever your age, and even when you have become a proficient swimmer, don't go into the water or on boats without the companionship of at least one expert swimmer. He serves as your lifeguard, and you act as his.

Boating can be great fun if you start in the proper way. First, try rowing, with an adult seated in the stern to guide you. You will find that pulling on a pair of oars gives your arms and legs a real workout. Next, try canoeing, with you seated in the stern and your adult companion in the prow. A canoe is the most graceful of small craft, and paddling one on a straight course is not difficult to learn.

Never stand up in a canoe; when changing places, crouch down and grasp the gunwales as you move along. For a wonderful feeling of relaxation, go sailing in one of the small boats that can be rented at many beaches. Never go boating in any kind of watercraft on the open ocean; confine your boating to streams, lakes, and protected coves. Learn nautical terms, knot tying, weather forecasting, and the fascinating "lore of the sea."

Suggested Paperback Books:

Young Sportsman's Guide to Swimming, Lynn Burke (New York: Cornerstone Library, Inc.), $1.00

Skin and Scuba Diving, Richard Hardwick (New York: Monarch Books), 50 cents

Beginning Skin and Scuba Diving, Councilman & Drinkwater (Belmont, Calif.: Wadsworth Publishing Co.), 75 cents

ABC's of Small Boat Handling, Lincoln and Alice Clark, Dolphin Books (Garden City, N.Y.: Doubleday & Co., Inc.), 95 cents

Suggested Hard-cover Books:

Young Sportsman's Guide to Diving, Robert L. Clotworthy (New York: Thomas Nelson & Sons), $2.75

Young Sportsman's Guide to Sailing, Wade H. De Fontaine (New York: Thomas Nelson & Sons), $2.75